Love-Based Online Marketing:

CAMPAIGNS TO GROW A BUSINESS YOU LOVE AND THAT LOVES YOU BACK

by Michele PW (Michele Pariza Wacek)

This book may be purchased for educational, business, or sales promotional use. For information, please email info@michelepw.com.

ISBN-10: 0-9968260-7-6
ISBN-13: 978-0-9968260-7-5

Library of Congress Number: 2016937895

DEDICATION

To all of you (you know who you are) who helped hold the space for me so I could get the Love-Based Philosophy out into the world.

xxoo

CONTENTS

Introduction

In 1998, I started my business as a freelance copywriter.

Now, if you know anything about service providers or freelancers, you know that despite what I just said, I started nothing of sort. What I started wasn't a business but a j-o-b.

And a terrible one at that.

I'd created a nightmare for myself. I was always overwhelmed and stressed, whether I was working like a nut writing copy and meeting with clients, or working like a nut trying to drum up more business because I had bills to pay.

It was feast or famine, baby. And mine was particularly brutal.

So, what was going wrong? Well, two things. First, despite the fact my business *was all about marketing* other people's business, I was doing a horrible job marketing my own.

That's the surface reason.

The deeper reason revolved around WHY I was doing such a rotten job marketing my business.

Unlike a lot of business owners and entrepreneurs, I not only know how to market myself, I also genuinely enjoy doing it. So, what was stopping me?

The easy answer is the joke we all tell — "the shoemaker's kids who have no shoes." But that isn't the reason either. (Keep reading — I'll tell you mine in just a bit.)

Here's the thing: If we aren't marketing ourselves the way we know we ought to be, there's something deeper going on. And that's what this book is about.

Yes, you'll find marketing strategies in this book, because not knowing what to do is a legitimate reason for not marketing yourself.

But, that's typically not the only reason. So, we're also going to delve into other reasons too.

Because all the strategy and knowledge and good intentions and "shoulds" in the world isn't worth a hill of beans if you haven't resolved the deeper issue, the REAL reason you aren't marketing yourself or your business.

Here's another example: Over the years, I've had clients pay me thousands of dollars for copy and marketing strategy and then never use any of it. When I would ask them why, the reasons they would give were usually around a mindset change, like deciding not to sell that particular product or program any longer, or even something more extreme, like deciding they didn't want to be in business anymore.

But that — changing their minds — wasn't the real reason they didn't use the marketing strategies or copy I'd given them.

The real reason is always something much deeper.

For myself, the real reasons — my deeper reasons — had to do with guilt, resentment, fear of failure, lack of boundaries and owning my value. (Note: multiple deeper reasons are not uncommon.)

It was only by working through those deeper issues was I able to start marketing my business on a regular basis, which not only led to the "smoothing out" of the feast and famine cycle, but also to my finally breaking 6 figures, and continuing to grow from there.

SO — if you're not happy with your business — you're not making the money you want to be; you're struggling to bring in clients or sales; it's not growing the way you had hoped; you're not getting your message out there or making the difference you want to be making — chances are, there's a problem with your marketing. It may be something internal that's blocking you, or something external, like a strategy or tactic that needs tweaking … or, it may be a combination of the two.

You'll find solutions to both of those — internal and external marketing blocks — in this book.

What Does Love-Based Online Marketing Even Mean?

In 2014, I came out with my first love-based book.

It was called "Love-Based Copywriting: How to Attract, Inspire and Invite Your Ideal Prospects to Become Ideal Clients."

From the beginning, it was a big success. People reached out to me about how much it changed their businesses and lives.

But, it also wasn't complete. I didn't take the content deep enough. And there were questions folks had that I didn't know they had, so I didn't answer them in the content. However, I didn't realize any of this until I went out and started promoting it by speaking on stages and on radio shows and podcasts.

I also realized I actually needed two books — one that focused on the philosophy of love-based copy (which is what the original book turned into, and I renamed it "Love-Based Copywriting Method: The Philosophy Behind Writing Copy That Attracts, Inspires and Invites") and a second book that focused on the nuts and bolts of copywriting (which I titled "Love-Based Copywriting System: A Step-by-Step Process to Writing Copy That Attracts, Inspires and Invites.")

In short, I ended up writing the second, editing the first, and releasing both. (If you want to check them out, you can do so right here: www.LoveBasedCopyBooks.com)

4

Along with getting the first two copywriting books sorted out, I came to another realization: *the love-based model could be applied to ALL parts of growing a business.*

Now, let's talk about love.

You see, there are only two "master" emotions — love and fear. All other emotions can be categorized under them.

Love-based emotions include love, hope, joy, gratitude, peace, faith, trust, confidence, happiness, connection, forgiveness, openness, passion, freedom, harmony, honesty, compassion, respect, acceptance, understanding, etc.

Fear-based emotions include fear, anger, grief, shame, guilt, bitterness, judgment, jealously, frustration, doubt, insecurity, etc.

How does this relate to business?

Well, because much of what we consider "traditional business" is built on a foundation of fear. Think about it: fear is easier. Many, many folks live their lives being controlled in some way by fear-based emotions. Either consciously — they're angry/depressed/grieving/judgmental/fearful/worrying/unhappy/etc., or unconsciously —and when they feel an uncomfortable emotion, they run away from it, bury it, hide from it, etc. (Consider all the things that happen when someone gets upset — he or she starts a fight, takes a drink, overeats, goes shopping, gossips, and so on.)

So, if fear-based emotions are controlling your behavior, it's going to be very difficult to build anything love-based.

Now, just to be clear, being love-based doesn't mean you don't feel fear-based emotions — on the contrary, people who have embraced love-based businesses and lives in fact DO fully feel all emotions, whether love-based or fear-based.

It simply means you lead with love-based emotions, and you don't allow fear-based emotions to dictate your actions.

It's important to realize that there IS definitely a place for fear-based emotions in our human existence. Whether we like it or not, fear-based emotions play an important role in our lives as humans.

Where we get into trouble is when we don't allow ourselves to really feel those emotions, because they don't feel good. That's when they tend to control us.

The key: rather than fight the fear-based emotions, you feel them and let them move through you. (Feelings just want to be felt, after all.)

You can then make decisions and take actions from a place of love. And you invite your ideal clients to do business with you by triggering love-based emotions versus fear-based.

(You can learn more about love-based and fear-based emotions and how both affect you and your business in my first love-based book "Love-Based Copywriting Method Volume 1"; I'm also releasing a "Love-Based Money and Mindset" book fall of 2016 that will go into this in more detail as well.)

Bottom line: You have a choice — you can choose to build your business on a foundation of love or you can build your business on a foundation of fear.

(A note about the "fear-based" terminology — it sounds super-judgmental, doesn't it? I don't actually mean it to, because I'm sincere about giving you a choice. But the problem is, fear-based businesses trigger fear-based emotions. That's what is going on, and for better or worse, that IS its name.)

What Does It Mean to Build a Business on a Foundation of Love?

That's the question I explore in my Love-Based Business series of books.

I believe if you want a love-based business, then every aspect of your business should be love-based — including (and especially) your marketing and your copy.

For example, the ways in which you bring your clients into your business sets the stage for your future relationship not only with those particular clients, but also with future clients. (Also, note that part of being love-based means not only are you inviting your clients in with love-based emotions, but that YOU also love what you've created — you love your marketing, your copy, your business, etc.)

Over time, you create a stronger brand doing business this way than when using fear-based tactics. When you bring people in using fear-based emotions, even if they didn't consciously know you did, they feet it. Some won't be bothered by that, but some will. And for those who are, that uncomfortable feeling will stick, and they may never feel completely at ease with you or your business from that point forward.

Also, fear-based marketing and copy tends to set the stage for more refunds than love-based, too, so keep in mind that even if gross sales are higher with fear-based, you may have a higher net with love-based because you'll have fewer refunds. And with higher refunds comes a larger pool of people who aren't happy with your business — hence the slow erosion of your brand.

Another important aspect of this is that love-based businesses allow people space to make a choice. You're committed to them taking action — but not attached to what that action should be.

Fear-based businesses are all about control. It's "my way or the highway." It's "If you don't buy my product, you're not only an idiot but your cat will die."

It's about chasing after potential customers to wrangle them in.

Love is about choice. Love is about educating and then standing back and giving people a choice around what they want to do. Just like I am educating you about love-based and fear-based tactics, and then stepping back so you can make the choice on which business you want to build.

(It really IS your choice. I'm simply here to educate you about your options.)

Again, in addition to marketing using the love-based philosophy, I also believe you truly need to love your marketing, if you want it to be authentically love-based.

I want you to *enjoy* your marketing. Have fun with it! WANT to do it.

And, yes, that's totally possible, even if you feel like you hate marketing right now. (If that's how you feel, don't worry; to help you identify the marketing activities you truly love doing, I've included a Love Your Marketing Assessment in Chapter 5, so be sure to complete it, when you get to it.)

The bottom line: the more relaxed you are, the more fun you're having, the more successful you'll be.

So, let's get this marketing party started!

Love-Based Online Marketing means attracting, inspiring and inviting your ideal prospects to become ideal clients. It means you're leading with love and other love-based emotions and giving your ideal clients space to make a choice. Love-Based Online Marketing also means you love your marketing as much as your ideal clients do!

How to Use This Book

Part 1 of this book has to do with your mindset, your inner game.

Pretty much everyone runs up against mindset blocks — the difference is just when. Some entrepreneurs hit a block the moment they ask for their first $100 sale, while others may be able to grow their business to $500K in record time, but then hit a ceiling they can't get beyond. Typically, when that happens, it means both mindset and strategies need to be up-leveled.

So, part one is designed to help you identify where you're stuck when it comes to marketing, and then, to give you some specific tips and exercises to get unstuck.

Part 2 is about marketing strategy.

I include some basic online marketing strategies and tactics to get yourself online and making money pretty quickly, and I also cover some advanced tips for after you've mastered the basics.

Part 3 provides a template for a marketing plan.

Now, when I say "marketing plan," I'm not talking about something complicated or confusing. I wanted to keep it simple for you, so it's easy to follow. This is pretty important, because if you don't follow your plan, it's not going to do you much good, right?

But if you have some sort of marketing and promotional plan in place, it's going to make it a lot easier to not only grow your business, but to also regulate your cash flow so you can eliminate the feast or famine cycle.

In addition, I've included exercises and action steps throughout the book to help you implement what you learn.

To really get the most out of the teachings, I would encourage you to actually roll up your sleeves and do the work as you read. It's the difference between watching someone demonstrate how to do pushups and actually doing the pushups. The demonstration may give you a lot of great tips, but you're not going to actually see much in the way of results.

So if you want to see the results, you probably want to do the work! ;)

The best part is, if you actually DO take a few minutes to work through the exercises as you read, by the time you complete the book, you will not only have a marketing plan you can begin to implement immediately, but you'll also have a handle on the blocks and resistances that have kept you from marketing your business the way your business (and gifts and message) really deserve.

There's a reason you have that burning desire to create, nurture and build your business. It's truly a disservice not only to yourself and your dreams, but everyone out there who needs what your business offers, if you don't learn how to successfully market and promote your business.

Lastly, I've also created a downloadable Love-Based Online Marketing Workbook to help guide you through the book. It will help you either create your marketing plan from scratch, or find the holes in your current plan. You can download your copy for free, here: www.lovebasedonlinemaketing.com/workbook

Part 1

YOUR INNER GAME/MARKETING MINDSET

Chapter 1
WHAT'S STOPPING YOU FROM MARKETING YOURSELF?

It's been said that owning your own business is one of the best personal development tools out there. (That and being a parent.)

It's my belief that marketing plays a big part in making it so.

Having a strong, thriving marketing arm is critical if you want a successful, profitable, sustainable business. In fact, it's so critical that entrepreneurs are often encouraged to wear two hats — a marketing hat, and a hat for whatever else the business sells.

But, here's the thing about marketing — for many, it's also a huge trigger.

Consider how marketing relates to the following common fears:

- Fear of success — marketing is key to business success.

- Fear of failure — marketing feels overwhelming, and what if it doesn't work? Example: "I'm not even going to try, because if I don't try, I won't fail."

- Money issues — marketing brings in revenue.

- Fear of not spending quality time with friends / family — marketing results in new clients, which sucks up time.

💜 Fear of visibility, or getting "big" — marketing gets you and your message "out there."

💜 Fear of owning your value — marketing shares your gifts and solutions with those who need you most. At least part of your message ought to be around the value you bring to your clients (and if it's not, it's probably not going to be very effective).

💜 Fear of having to "sell" yourself — marketing often brings in prospects who simply need a conversation with you in order to become a client.

This short list doesn't even touch on the other reasons entrepreneurs struggle with marketing — things like not enjoying marketing in and of itself, not having the time to market themselves, not wanting to feel slimy or sales-y, not wanting to be like the slimy marketers out there who are only about "getting the sale," or just not having the experience or knowledge when it comes to marketing best practices.

It's no wonder why marketing is one of the biggest challenges entrepreneurs experience, and why it brings up so much resistance on so many different levels.

Resistance, by the way, is something that Steven Pressfield talks about in his book "War of Art." Basically, every time you make moves to expand and grow as a person, resistance will rear its ugly head to stop you. It's not personal; it's the human condition, and it happens to everyone. (Interesting enough, the converse never happens, so if you're descending and becoming a worse human being, you'll get no resistance to stop you. It's only when you're trying to ascend and become a better human.)

So, if owning a business is one of the best personal development tools you have, and the point of your personal development journey is to become a better human (to clarify, I'm not talking about the point of having a business, which of course is to create an excellent income for yourself while making a difference, traveling the world, having time for your family, etc. — whatever is important to you and why you started your business — I'm simply talking about your business as a way to help you grow as a person) then of course, resistance is going to come up.

And, as marketing is the lifeblood of any business, it's easy to understand how marketing could easily become a mirror to the blocks, fears, doubts, resistance, etc. that you have around growing as a person, and fulfilling your dreams and purpose. Right?

Here's the great news: knowing this, you are now in a perfect position to uncover the resistance and blocks you're experiencing, and move through them.

How?

Well, to start, get a handle as to *where* marketing resistance shows up for you.

Here's an exercise that can help, but first:

Be warned: marketing resistance can be awfully sneaky. It's not uncommon to discover multiple resistances, as well as hidden resistances, or to even have resistances disguise themselves as something else altogether. (Why would they do that? So you can't work through and release them. If you think you're dealing with one thing and it's actually something else, it can remain a block inside you.)

That's exactly why I recommend reading all the chapters of this book, even if you think you don't need one. You may have a "hidden" resistance in an area you aren't even aware of yet.

Also, completing the following exercise may not reveal ALL of your resistances, and that's okay. You have to start somewhere. Sometimes, you need to deal with the "surface" blocks before you can even see the deeper ones. So, wherever you are right now, or however this shows up for you is perfect, just as it is.

EXERCISE

This is a journaling exercise. I recommend using pen and paper versus typing on a computer, because when you write by hand, you are more likely to tap into deeper levels of your subconscious — but of course, do what feels right for you. (Remember to download my Love-Based Online Marketing Workbook, which provides space for you to complete the following exercise. You can do that now, here: www.lovebasedonlinemaketing.com/workbook)

Take a few moments to answer the following questions honestly, without censoring yourself. Don't overthink, just write. And write down EVERYTHING you can think of, for each question.

1. How do I feel about marketing in general?

2. How do I feel about myself when I market myself?

3. What is my number one frustration/dislike around marketing, and why?

4. Now, make a list of 3-4 other marketing-related frustrations/dislikes. For each, also ask yourself why it bothers you, and write down the reasons. (Consider this a mini-brainstorming session, and write whatever comes to mind.)

5. Revisit number 4 above two or three times to make sure you capture as many of your resistances as you can on paper.

Now, as I mentioned earlier, this list may not be complete, or there may be something on your list that's actually disguising itself as something else, so it's not really showing itself yet … but completing this exercise gives you a solid start.

Take a look at everything on your list. If you're like a lot of folks, you probably have multiple dislikes or frustrations around marketing. Marketing is a pretty big trigger, for most people.

And because it's a trigger, it's important to identify the resistances we have about marketing first — before we can anything about releasing them.

Next up: I'm covering the most common reasons people have for feeling averse to marketing. I may not have your exact, specific reason, but hopefully I'll cover something in the same neighborhood — and you can apply those same tips and action steps to your specific resistance, so you can start working through it.

And the best part? A lot of marketing resistance is tied to success in general, so by working through this now, you'll likely find yourself attracting more success in all areas of your life, not just business. Remember, resistance shows up in all sorts of ways in order to prevent you from getting the work done you know you're meant to. So you may find yourself procrastinating or not being able to focus or attracting all sorts of drama or getting sick or something else. But once the resistance goes away, many of those obstacles also start melting away, which then paves the way for you to build a successful business.

So, let's get started.

Chapter 2
DON'T LIKE/DON'T UNDERSTAND/DON'T HAVE TIME/ALL MARKETERS ARE CON ARTISTS

I'm starting off with the "easy" reasons why people struggle with marketing. (When I say "easy" here, I'm referring to the fact that these are the easiest fixes.)

So, let's start by examining the reason (which is of course, the resistance), and then immediately following, the various solutions.

Resistance 1: I Don't Like Marketing

What???? How can you not like marketing?

Okay, so yes, I'm a marketing geek. And yes, there is a part of me that just doesn't get *why* you don't love marketing or *how* you couldn't!

But, sigh … I do understand that marketing isn't everyone's cup of tea.

And, quite honestly, even if you DO enjoy marketing, you probably enjoy what your business actually does — the solution you provide — more. (Unless, of course, your business IS marketing.)

So, what do you if you don't like marketing?

21

Well, first off, I would challenge that there is probably SOMETHING that is connected to marketing you WOULD enjoy. There are sooooo many ways to market yourself that there is at least one way you could probably get behind.

To help you find your marketing "sweet spot," be sure to take my "Love Your Marketing Assessment" in Chapter 5. And even if you DO enjoy marketing, you'll still want to take the assessment — I bet there are some marketing activities you enjoy more than others, and this will help you determine what they are.

Now, the best part of identifying your Marketing Love is that it's not only going to be the activity you most enjoy, but also the one you're likely best at doing. AND it's probably also the one that's going to get you the most bang for your buck. So if you focus ONLY on your Marketing Love, you're likely to start to see your biggest returns.

Of course, a well-rounded marketing plan will include activities that are not your fave and/or you're not particularly good at, too. That's okay — that's why you hire a team.

A reliable team can focus on all the other marketing activities you don't necessarily enjoy or have time for, freeing you up to focus on what you do best. And once you ARE focused on — and doing — your Marketing Love, the money will most likely follow, which means you'll have the cash flow to support your team.

ACTION STEPS:

- 💜 Take the Assessment in Chapter 5 — Love Your Marketing (but don't jump ahead quite yet, wait until you actually get to that chapter).

- 💜 Hire a Reliable Team — one that loves marketing (or who loves the marketing activities you don't love), so your marketing actually gets done.

RESISTANCE 2: I DON'T UNDERSTAND MARKETING

Variations include feeling:

- 💜 Like you don't have the experience, knowledge, expertise, etc. you need to do anything.

- 💜 Overwhelmed by the myriad strategies and tactics thrown at you (Do Facebook ads! Start a podcast! Write more blog posts!), so you don't know where to start or which is right for you.

- 💜 Stuck — like you can't even get started until you read "one more book."

First off, take a deep breath.

This book is going to give you a basic knowledge and understanding of marketing AND walk you through how to put together a marketing strategy that's right for you. I designed it to get as many of your strategy and tactical questions answered as possible.

Now, this particular "I don't understand marketing" resistance could be one of those sneaky masqueraders, hiding a deeper resistance. For example, overwhelm could be a common theme in your life when you're stuck on something. Or, maybe you're using your lack of marketing knowledge to "get ready to get ready." In these cases, we'd need to dig a little deeper.

So, how do you know if this particular reason is masquerading, and is really a deeper resistance?

Start by reading this book in its entirety. As you go through each chapter, pay attention to your reactions and feelings. If you read something that strikes a bolt of lightning in you — regardless of whether it's around something you know you need to do or around something you're completely repelled by (or both), it's probably a sign there's something else going on, so make note of it.

ACTION STEPS:

- Keep Reading and Completing the Exercises — even if you think they don't "apply" to you. Know as you keep reading, you WILL get the marketing knowledge you need.

RESISTANCE 3: I DON'T HAVE TIME FOR MARKETING

Ah, my old, familiar friend. I, too, didn't have time for marketing.

Now, while it's true that when I was a freelancer, I was extremely busy (typically working 6-7 days a week), it's also true that I didn't choose to make marketing a priority. And the reason I didn't was because I felt like I needed to put my clients' needs first.

This sounds all well and good on the surface, but it's sort of like what they tell you on the plane if the oxygen masks suddenly appear — put yours on first before you assist others. And it makes perfect sense, right? You can't help anyone if you're passed out on the floor.

The reality is, by not taking care of my own business and making sure my cash flow was consistent so I could take care of my own needs, how on earth could I possibly be completely present for my clients?

Not to mention being completely out of integrity — I know we all laugh at the cobbler's kids who don't have shoes story, but now that I've been there, I feel like your business needs to be integrity with what you're offering. (Note: this doesn't mean it has to be perfect all the time, or that you can't help people who are making more money than you. You just need to make sure your side of the street is cleaned up, so to speak.)

The point I'm making is, in my opinion, the time excuse, while being a real concern, IS truly an excuse. Because we always make time for what is important to us, and if we're not making time for something we think is important, it's either really not as important as we think, or there's some other block or resistance going on.

The easy answer here is if you don't have time, hire someone to do your marketing for you. Marketing really is something that will pay for itself, so it's easier to justify hiring someone to help in this area then, say, bookkeeping. (As important as bookkeeping is, it's still mostly an administrative function and doesn't actually result in money flowing into the business.) Also, if you are so busy you don't have the time to market yourself, then you probably are making enough money to justify the hire.

But, if you really feel like you don't have either the time or the money to hire someone (even a couple hundred dollars for a few hours of a virtual assistant's time a month), then something else is going on. There's some reason you aren't prioritizing marketing — and by not doing so, you're putting the success of your business in jeopardy. That's why we need to get to the bottom of it — so you can start reaping the benefit of consistently (and effectively) marketing yourself.

ACTION STEPS:

- 💜 Get Crystal Clear — Do you really not have the time? Or are you simply not making the time?

- 💜 Consider Hiring Help — If you truly don't have time, this is one of the best investments you can make in your biz, even if it's just a few hours a month. (After you put your marketing plan together, you'll have a better idea of where you need the help, how much help you need, and who you need to hire.)

- 💜 Dig a Little Deeper — If you're simply not making the time, dig a little deeper and figure out why. Is it because you simply don't like marketing? Or is there something deeper going on? If there is something deeper going on, I recommend working on that first. You may also want to look into hiring a team, but if you don't get rid of your blocks, it's going to be difficult to enjoy consistent success around marketing even if you do have a team.

RESISTANCE 4: I THINK ALL MARKETERS / INTERNET MARKETERS ARE CON ARTISTS AND SLIMEBALLS

If this resistance is coming up for you, the problem isn't so much that you think marketers are slimy, but that YOU don't want to be slimy when you're marketing yourself.

I *get* it.

Who wants to be considered slimy, sleazy or a con artist?

Yet, when you feel this way, it's very difficult (if not impossible) to actually market yourself properly, because subconsciously you don't want to become slimy or sleazy. You end up unconsciously and/or subconsciously sabotaging yourself when it comes to marketing your business, which of course means you never find yourself attracting consistent success.

Okay, so let's dig into this a little deeper. First of all, you're not entirely wrong. There most certainly ARE marketers out there who are sleazy, slimy con artists. But, for the most part, the true con artists are definitely in the minority.

However, what you may be reacting to is something I call fear-based marketing. Remember, as I mentioned earlier, a lot of traditional marketing and copy is based on triggering fear-based emotions — fear, shame, guilt, anger, etc.

The marketers who use fear-based marketing aren't necessarily bad people — in my experience, they tend to be pretty pragmatic (fear-based works, so why re-invent the wheel?), and they tend to believe the end justifies the means. In other words, they don't necessarily care HOW you get people to buy a product, just as long as they DO buy. And, in a lot of cases, it's because they believe so strongly in their product and program they know if people try it, they'll receive the transformation.

Alas, that's not how it works. (At least, in my opinion.)

I cover this in detail in Volume 1 of the Love-Based Business series, "Love-Based Copywriting Method: The Philosophy Behind Writing Copy That Attracts, Inspires and Invites."

(Note: I know the title of the book above is about copy [because copy is what is actually doing the triggering] but it also applies to marketing and marketing triggers. So, if you want to learn the philosophy and triggers of love-based marketing, that book will lay it all out for you.)

In a nutshell, traditional direct response marketing and copy is based on triggering fear-based emotions, which is why it feels so "yucky."

So, it's my suspicion that some of that "all marketers are sleazy" feeling is backlash from years and years of fear-based marketing. I also suspect this will change if and when more and more businesses move to love-based marketing and copy, and *those* examples start to populate the Internet.

When you realize that you have a choice — that you can choose to market yourself with love by triggering love-based emotions (love, abundance, hope, connection, respect) instead of fear — not only will you feel much more in alignment with your marketing, but you'll also help "rehabilitate" the slimy image most folks have of marketing right now.

(Another way to think about all of this is that internet marketing/ marketing is simply a tool — it isn't inherently good or bad or slimy or sales-y or anything else. What makes it feel good or bad or manipulative or whatever is the person behind the tool. I know it's easy to confuse the person who is handling the tool with the tool itself, but if you can keep this in mind, it's easier to see how the person behind the tool makes the choice.)

ACTION STEPS:

- 💜 Commit — If you resonate with the love-based copy and marketing approach, make a commitment right now to begin marketing your business by triggering love-based emotions instead of fear. Since you aren't marketing yourself like those "other" slimy marketers, eventually this resistance should start melting away.

- 💜 Go a Little Deeper — Ask yourself (or do some journaling) around why you think marketers are slimy. What exactly makes them that way? What bothers you so much about them? Don't leave anything out — get it all out on paper. Once you do that, look at what you wrote. Then, ask yourself: Is it "true?" How do you know if it's "true?" You may want to use Byron Katie's exercise (more on that in Chapter 3) to really root around and get at the cause as to why you feel the way you do about marketers, which will help you finally let it go.

Now that we've covered some of the more "surface level" blocks and resistances to marketing, we're ready to move into the "deeper" blocks.

Let's go!

Chapter 3
FEAR OF SUCCESS/FEAR OF FAILURE/ MONEY AND MORE

Now it's time to delve into some of the deeper, murkier resistances that you may not even be completely consciously aware of right now, because they have a tendency to bury deep. Alas, these are also the ones that are probably stopping you the most, so getting a handle on them is pretty important, if you want to move forward in your marketing.

(Note: While you will find exercises and action steps in this chapter for each one of these, if you find you're truly stuck, you may want to enlist the help of a coach who specializes in getting rid of blocks and resistance. You can find some excellent resources here: www.lovebasedbooks.com/resources)

RESISTANCE 1: I HATE SELLING / I HATE SELLING MYSELF

The question really is — *why* do you hate selling?

Is it because you think sales people are all slimy and sales-y? (See "I Think All Marketers Are Con Artists and Slimeballs" in previous chapter.)

Is it because you're having issues valuing yourself and your gifts?

Is it because you're struggling with making money?

All of the above? Something else?

It's important to get to the bottom of this one.

Chances are, hating selling isn't really the problem. The problem is what selling *represents* to you.

EXERCISE

That's right — it's time to journal again. Get some paper and a pen. Center yourself by sitting quietly for a few minutes and taking a few deep breaths. Now, start journaling around the question "Why do I hate selling?"

Don't censor yourself, just let it all out. What exactly is blocking you — no matter how silly or insignificant you think it is. You can use the questions above to help you brainstorm your answers.

When you think you're done, take a breath, and then keep writing for a few more minutes. (Usually the gold happens after you think you've exhausted everything there is to say on this topic, so keep going, just a little longer.) You may want to do this a few times to really make sure you get it all out onto the paper.

Once you're done, take a moment to read and review what you wrote. Are you seeing any themes? Make a note of them.

- If while you complete this exercise, a different resistance surfaces, don't worry. Simply review the corresponding section of the new resistance, and work through those action steps. This is totally normal!

RESISTANCE 2: I'M GETTING READY TO GET READY

So, I suspect that's not exactly what you're saying to yourself — your inner dialog probably sounds something more along the lines of:

- ❤ "I need to finish my schooling/earn my certification/finish this class/read one more book and then I'll be ready,"

OR

- ❤ "I need to finish my book/finish my program/finish my website and then I'll be ready,"

OR

- ❤ "I need to get my ducks in a row before I can do X,"

OR

- ❤ "I need to wait until the kids are in school/out of school/moved out/moved back in and then I can do X."

Basically, these are all variations of the same resistance: needing X to be in place before you can do Y.

On the surface, this actually makes a lot of sense and can be easily justified. But scratch a little deeper, and you'll find what's really going on: it's a delaying technique.

How do you know if this is what's happening with you?

Read the following, and pay attention to your reactions as you do:

- You keep adding to the ever-growing list of things that need to be in place for Y to happen. For instance, maybe you wanted to get certified as a coach before you started your business. But, then you decided you needed to take a marketing class. And then you realized you needed to get your website done, but, oh, you'd better take a Wordpress class so you can build your site, and then, you had to take a copywriting course to write your copy FOR the website. And, before you actually launched your site, you had to get professional pictures taken, but before you did that, you wanted to lose twenty pounds ... and on and on.

My point: You don't really need ANY of that to line up a few clients and start coaching. (Yes, even the actual certification. Now don't get me wrong; I think getting coaching training is an excellent thing, and personally, I continuously educate myself on my craft — but I don't allow it to stand in my way of finding paying clients.) So, while all of the things I mentioned will help you run a successful business, none of it needs to be in place to get started.

- You never finish X so you can't do Y. I see this a lot when it comes to writing books. "I have to do one final edit of my book, and then I can launch my book and my business."

Sounds simple enough, sure. Except what happens when it's suddenly been three years, and you still haven't done that "one final edit"?

If you recognize yourself in either of these scenarios (or maybe in a little of both) then alas, you are stuck in the "getting ready to get ready phase."

So, what do you do to get out of it?

Well, once again, I suspect there's a deeper resistance going on that's actually stopping you. The "getting ready to get ready" excuse is simply a way to justify staying stuck — to not move forward.

ACTION STEPS:

- Complete the Journaling Exercise in the "I Hate Selling" section above, if you haven't already — and see what surfaces for you that's keeping you stuck in "getting ready to get ready."

37

RESISTANCE 3: WOULD BAD THINGS HAPPEN IF I WERE A SUCCESS?

Other variations of this include:

- ❤ "How would my spouse feel if I were more successful than he/she is?"

- ❤ "Will my spouse leave me if I'm more successful?"

- ❤ "How will my family react if I'm a success? Will they still love and support me?"

- ❤ "I can't be more successful than my parents."

- ❤ "I don't want to be successful because successful people have no time and I'll end up ignoring my family."

- ❤ "I don't deserve success."

- ❤ "Who am I to believe I should be successful?"

- ❤ "I'm really full of myself and/or ungrateful if I try and be more successful."

In other words, you're likely experiencing this resistance if you feel like you don't want, shouldn't want, or don't deserve success.

> "Our deepest fear is not that we are inadequate. Our deepest fear is that we are powerful beyond measure. It is our light, not our darkness that most frightens us."
>
> — Marianne Williamson

I suspect this one — the fear of success — is more common than we really want to admit.

I also suspect that even the most successful entrepreneurs out there at some point struggled with a fear of success (and some probably still do, which often keeps them from breaking through to the next level of success).

So know you're not alone.

Of course, knowing that doesn't help you actually move forward. So what do you do?

The problem with a lot of the resistances that fall under the "umbrella" of fear of success — and, for that matter, those that fall under money or value or visibility — is that they're pretty deep. They may even be considered part of your "core beliefs." Because they're so deep, it may take time and possibly a few different approaches before you can really work your way through them.

So, the first thing I want you to do is be patient with yourself. These deep beliefs didn't happen overnight, and they probably won't disappear overnight.

Second, I've included a few different exercises and approaches you can try at the end of this chapter to move through these resistances (in fact, you can use them to begin eliminating any and all deeper resistances that bubble up for you).

ACTION STEPS:

- Complete the Exercises at the end of this chapter to begin moving through your resistance in this area.

RESISTANCE 4: WOULD BAD THINGS HAPPEN IF I STARTED MAKING MORE MONEY?

Ah, now we're getting into a big one — money stuff.

One of my teachers once told me that there are three big mirrors that will always reflect your own "stuff" right back at you: money, health and relationships.

What does that mean, exactly?

Well, let's say your mirror is health. If you're ignoring your intuition and moving forward on something your intuition is telling you not to do, you may find that you end up getting sick.

Basically, one of those main categories acts as a mirror for other issues you're dealing with. You chronically ignore what your intuition tells you, and you chronically get sick. You may think you have health problems, but what's really going on is that your health is just the mirror, not the actual issue. Once you start listening to and respecting your gut, you'll stop getting sick.

Circling back to money, now: money brings along its own baggage and issues, sure … but it can also act as a mirror for other issues in your life.

No wonder money is such a touchy and triggering subject, right?

As with some of the other resistances, this one has a whole bunch of variations including:

- ❤ "Who am I to charge this much?"

- ❤ "Money is the root of all evil."

- ❤ "Rich people are evil/greedy/out to get me/etc."

- ❤ "What will happen if I make more money than my parents? Would they still love me?"

- ❤ "What will happen if I make more money than my spouse? Would my spouse leave me?"

💜 "If I start making more money, that must mean I'll have to work all the time and ignore my family."

💜 "If I really love what I'm doing, I shouldn't be charging for it."

💜 "I'm a good person and I'm trying to transform the world — I shouldn't be charging for that."

💜 "I'm spiritual so money shouldn't be important to me."

Whew! It's no wonder we struggle so much with money!

All of these variances can be roughly grouped into a few categories:

1. Money as related to your value/worth (i.e. "Who am I to charge this much?")

2. Money as related to family/community/love (i.e. "Will my family stop loving me/leave me if I make more money?")

3. Money as related to culture (i.e. "Rich people are evil.")

Now, let's look at these a little more closely.

💜 Money as related to your value/worth: If you don't value your gifts or feel like you "should" be charging for sharing them, then *any* sort of marketing and selling is going to be painfully difficult for you. After all, how can you possibly ask for money if you secretly feel like you don't deserve it? And, even if someone gives you money, aren't you going to still feel like you don't deserve it? This will clearly impact your ability to attract a regular flow of money into your life.

💜 Money as related to family/community/love: If you feel deep down that you have to choose between having love or money in your life, chances are you're going to choose love — which means you will also unconsciously sabotage your own efforts to attract money.

💜 Money as related to culture: If you feel like rich people are evil and money is evil, why on earth would you want to attract more money into your life? So you could become an evil, greedy rich person too? If you feel like you're a good person, you're going to attract the exact amount of money that allows you to still feel like you're a good person, and no more. (And, no, you can't predetermine this — "Well, I'm sure I'll still be a good person if I break 6 figures — it's only if I start making millions." First of all, you don't know what number your subconscious has in mind — but if you haven't broken 6 figures yet, it's likely not 6 figures — and second of all, just by *thinking* that rich people are evil and greedy, you're going to throttle back attracting money on all levels. Money is the same energy as all energy: it goes where it's wanted and cherished, not where it's put down and criticized.)

Now, just to be clear, in many cases, the ways in which you're blocking the flow of money to yourself is unconscious — you don't see how you're sabotaging yourself. For instance, you could have one of these money blocks, but the way it's showing up is that you're not marketing yourself properly. And, when you're asked why you're not marketing yourself properly, you say "Well, I hate to market myself," or "I think all marketers are slimy," or "I have no time to market myself."

So, the real problem isn't that you hate marketing or think all marketers are slimy or that you don't have enough time to market yourself. The REAL resistance is deeper — maybe you feel if you make too much money, your spouse will leave you.

See how those "surface" blocks hide the real, deeper ones?

ACTION STEPS:

- 💜 Complete the Exercises at the end of this chapter to begin moving through your resistance in this area.

(Because money is such a massive topic, I'm devoting an entire book to money and mindset: "Love-Based Money and Mindset." You can learn more here: www.LoveBasedCopyBooks.com)

RESISTANCE 5: WILL BAD THINGS HAPPEN IF I FAIL?

This is "fear of failure," and it covers things like what people might think, whether your family/loved ones would leave you, what you would do, who you think you would be etc. if you failed.

Now, you may be thinking; "Why is fear of failure here? If you have a fear of failing in your business, doesn't that mean you'll throw yourself into marketing because that's been proven to help businesses be successful?"

Well, yes — that may be one way fear of failure manifests itself (overworking is another common manifestation of this one).

But another way fear of failure manifests itself is when it keeps you stuck, because you simply don't try.

After all, how can you fail if you don't even try?

So, you absolutely DON'T want to market yourself, because (perhaps subconsciously, even) you're thinking "What if I throw everything into marketing, and I STILL fail? What does that say about me then? That I really am a loser? And who AM I if I fail at this?"

You can see how it could easily feel safer to not even try — that way you can't fail, and then you'll never have to face the fact that your inner critic was actually right all along.

Luckily, there's another way. You don't have to be held hostage by your fear of failure anymore.

ACTION STEPS:

💜 Complete the Exercises at the end of this chapter to begin moving through your resistance in this area.

RESISTANCE 6: WOULD BAD THINGS HAPPEN IF I WERE "OUT THERE" IN A BIG WAY?

This is fear of being visible, becoming famous, "getting big" or being seen.

And it's a super-common fear to have.

After all, the more well-known and famous you are, the more vulnerable you are, right? And the more you open yourself up to more criticism, judgments, and other hateful things you know people will say.

Maybe you're worried about being embarrassed, because you feel uncomfortable in the spotlight, and being more visible means more spotlight.

On top of that, you may have insecurities around your value —
who are YOU to be so visible — to be famous? Or worries about
how your family will react if you become famous. Or maybe you
have safety issues around being famous and visible. Or maybe,
there's something else driving you to stay small and invisible.

Since the point of marketing is to get the word out about yourself,
clearly any sort of block you have around visibility/being famous is
going to get triggered pretty heavily here.

It's okay! Take a deep breath, and remember there really is light at
the end of the tunnel.

ACTION STEPS:

♥ Complete the Exercises at the end of this chapter to
begin moving through your resistance in this area.

RESISTANCE 7: I'M A FRAUD

I remember being at an event where one of the presenters told a
story about how he had been feeling like a fraud — he had all this
visibility, with television shows and other promotions, so from the
outside, it looked like his business was kicking butt. But, the reality
was, he was barely paying his bills.

In the middle of this difficult period, he had the chance to speak
with a woman who had just been nominated for the Nobel Peace

prize. During the conversation, he ended up telling her how much of a fraud he felt like he was. Her answer: "I feel like a fraud too!"

The point here being is that an extremely high percentage of the highly-successful people I know (including myself) have confessed to, at one point or another, feeling like a fraud, and/or thinking "Others are going to find out the truth about me, and then what?"

So, if you too feel like a fraud, you're in very good company.

However, it can be tough to market yourself when you are feeling like a fraud because, well, how on earth can you get behind selling yourself and your business when you feel like you're a big phony? And if you DO get there, wouldn't you then be just like those slimy con artist marketers out there? At the very least, wouldn't you then be out of integrity?

Ah, the tangled webs we weave when we start encountering and confronting our resistances!

Now, if it makes you feel any better, I will tell you that the sheer fact you're worrying about being a fraud is probably a strong indication that you're not one. You see, people who are truly frauds rarely think about it, much less worry about it. Only people with integrity worry about being frauds, because being a fraud means you're out of integrity. If integrity isn't all that high on your list of values, this really isn't much of a concern.

And, for those of you who have this particular resistance so bad that I can pretty much hear you saying: "But Michele — I'M different and I really AM a fraud" … before you even go there, take a deep breath and start going through the exercises below.

You see, there's a dirty little secret here, which is this: everyone has moments when he or she is out of integrity. And you know what? It doesn't matter. It doesn't mean you don't have anything to offer the world. And it doesn't mean you can't fix whatever you're out of integrity with, and get yourself back on track. (Remember my story? I was in the business of marketing other people, and I wasn't marketing myself. If you looked at what I was doing for myself, you would never have hired me — but that didn't mean I didn't know what I was doing. And, I suspect the same could apply to you.)

ACTION STEPS TO HELP YOU THROUGH DEEPER RESISTANCE

Below, I've included 4 different exercises designed to help you break through whatever resistance is coming up for you — whichever blocks you're confronting.

I encourage you to try all four, and if you're feeling called, I also encourage you to try other modalities and coaches. Not all personal development exercises work (or work the same) for all people. So, if you choose to walk down this path of working through your mindset blocks, I encourage you to stay open, and see what does and doesn't resonate with you. (Keep in mind I will be coming out with a "Love-Based Money and Mindset" book in 2016, which is all about shifting your mindset to one of abundance, and how to attract more abundance into your life and business. Plus, it'll include more exercises to help you with your marketing blocks. Check out www.LoveBasedCopyBooks.com to learn more about when it will be available.)

In addition, (and this is important!), if there's an exercise you absolutely don't want to have anything to do with, I suggest you start with that one. You may even want to focus on it. I know, it feels counterintuitive … but if you really don't want to do it, that's probably a good sign that it's exactly what you need to do to break through your biggest blocks.

Lastly, remember that these exercises have been designed to provide "maximum impact." You may choose to work on your money blocks and find that you're also clearing some relationship blocks in the process. You may discover you stop worrying as much, or your level of anxiety drops, or you're far more peaceful than you were before completing these exercises. In other words, you may discover that you get a lot more benefit from practicing these exercises than you were even hoping for. Such is the beauty of "doing the work"!

EXERCISE 1 — BREATHING

I have a confession — for years I would roll my eyes every time I heard any of that "stop and breathe" advice.

But I've recently delved into the whole breathing thing more deeply, and there's a trick to it.

The trick: you need to feel your feelings.

The idea is, whenever uncomfortable or unpleasant thoughts come up, you pause whatever you're doing and *breathe into* the emotions surrounding the unpleasant thoughts.

You see, feelings just want to be felt. However, if they're based in fear, like worry, anger, guilt, shame, anxiety, etc., they're probably uncomfortable, and you likely don't *want* to feel them. So, you stuff them down or run away from them or ignore them altogether.

Alas, that doesn't actually make them go away. If you want them to go away, you need to take the time to really feel them.

Here's how this would work:

Let's say you have a marketing task on your to-do list, like writing a blog post. But, instead of writing that blog post, you find yourself procrastinating and doing anything BUT writing that blog post.

So first, pause. Close your eyes, and breathe into that procrastination feeling inside you.

Just feel it. Breathe into it. And see what comes up.

51

The first time you do this, you may find it very unpleasant, because you're confronting the unpleasant emotion head-on. But, if you keep it up, you'll find that it not only gets easier and easier, but even better, that your blocks and resistance slowly begin melting away. (Really! You don't have to do anything else but feel the emotion.)

EXERCISE 2 — BREAK THE CYCLE

(Note — this is a good one to do if breathing into your emotions is too intense or difficult for you.)

This exercise is contributed by a good friend of mine, Therese Skelly, who is an expert at identifying your core message, and releasing the blocks that keep you from success, so you can make the difference you're here to make.

But first, full disclosure: Therese is the one who let me know that my first exercise — breathing and letting yourself feel your emotions — is actually more of an advanced tactic. (Although it certainly sounds pretty simple, doesn't it?)

Why is it considered advanced? Well, if you have some serious trauma in your past that you haven't dealt with, or if you've never really allowed yourself to feel your unpleasant emotions, the first time you try it this technique could be a massive shock to your system. (I know the first time I tried it, I felt so awful I thought I was going to die. No kidding, I felt horrible and sick, to the point of assuming I must be doing it wrong: how could something that felt so bad be good for me? But after I moved past that, my anxiety level significantly dropped.)

So, if jumping into the deep end isn't your style, you may want to back your way in a bit more slowly: by breaking the cycle that normally occurs when you stumble upon a mindset block, and then, rewiring your brain for a different reaction.

Here's how it works:

Let's say you have a fear of being seen. And let's say out of the blue, you get an email inviting you to speak on stage in front of an audience filled with your ideal clients. It's even being hosted by a well-respected expert in your industry, so just by standing on that stage, you know you're going to benefit from a ton of credibility.

Sounds like a dream come true, right?

But, you have a fear of being seen. And, if you get on that stage, you will most definitely be seen.

Which means, that subconscious block kicks in.

So, what happens then?

Well, you're most likely going to have an external and an internal reaction.

Externally, it may look like this: you procrastinate replying back to the person, so you lose the speaking opportunity altogether. Or if you do get the gig, you procrastinate putting your talk together until the very last minute, so you end up staying up all night and subsequently giving a poor talk. Or, maybe you don't even make it on the stage, because you end up losing your voice or getting a bad case of the flu.

Internally, it may look like this: the closer you get to the date of your talk, the more anxious and nervous you become. Maybe you stop being able to sleep, or you end up binging on food or alcohol, or you're just cranky and irritable.

The internal reaction is what is driving the external results — which in this case means you end up either not giving the talk at all (because you never replied or you got sick) or it's not a very good one (because you procrastinated putting your talk together and/or didn't take good care of yourself so your energy was lousy on stage).

Now, if you want to prevent the external reaction, what you need to do is stop the internal reaction. And the way to do that is when you start to feel yourself slipping into anxiousness or worry or fear or irritability, you recognize it, and do something to break that physical reaction. Maybe you have a mantra you can repeat, or someone you can call who can intervene and "talk you down" (it's important to note that this is not the same as gossiping or complaining about it — this is simply a sympathetic ear who will help diffuse the situation for you before your emotions spiral out of control), or maybe you use Emotional Freedom Technique (also called EFT or tapping).

Once you're able to stop the physical reaction, you can start to break the cycle between the fear you have (in this case, the fear of being seen) and how you're sabotaging your marketing. And, once you've broken that cycle, you can start to rewire or re-pattern your brain, so that you don't automatically go into fear or anxiety or worry or anger when you bump into mindset blocks.

(If you'd like to learn more about how to find your message and get it out into the world, see the Resource section to get Therese's free gift: **"Blind Spot to Brilliance: Marketing from the Inside Out" eBook.**)

EXERCISE 3 — WHAT'S THE WORST THAT COULD HAPPEN?

Another exercise Therese recommends for dissolving resistance is to play the fear out. That's right — play it out to either its logical conclusion, or beyond that to its absolute worst possible outcome.

Here's how this works:

First, make sure you've clearly defined your fear. So, if you haven't done the journaling exercise in Chapter 1 to get really clear on your exact, specific fear, start by doing that.

Once you've identified the specific fear, start playing it out to the very end, by asking yourself probing questions.

For instance, let's say you have a fear of being seen. You'd ask yourself a series of questions like the following:

- So what are you afraid is going to happen when you're seen? Maybe someone will criticize me.

- So, what's the worst that will happen if someone criticizes you? Well, it means they don't like me.

- So, what's the worst that will happen if someone doesn't like you? Well, maybe they'll say mean things and try and hurt my business.

- So, what's the worst that will happen if someone says mean things and tries to hurt your business? Well, maybe they actually will hurt my business.

- So, what's the worst that will happen if someone hurts your business? Well, maybe I'll go out of business.

- So, what's the worst that will happen if you go out of business? Well, maybe I'll need to go get a job.

Okay, so you can see how this goes. You can keep going from there — all the way from not being able to find a job to losing all your money and ending up homeless and on the street. All because you allowed yourself to be seen.

For some people, the sheer act of going through this exercise allows them to see how baseless and (dare I say it?) silly their actual fear is, which allows them to start moving past it.

EXERCISE 4 — BYRON KATIE'S "THE WORK"

If you're not familiar with Byron Katie or "The Work," I invite you to check out her website where she lays out this exercise in its entirety for free at TheWork.com.

I'll just give you the basics here.

"The Work" is a way to question the truth to the stories we're telling ourselves.

So, let's say we have the story "If I make too much money, my spouse will leave me."

You begin by writing that on a piece of paper, and then, you journal the answers to the following four questions:

1. Is it true? (Yes or no. If no, move to 3.)

2. Can you absolutely know that it's true? (Yes or no.)

3. How do you react, what happens, when you believe that thought?

4. Who would you be without that thought?

Then, you turn around the original statement and answer the questions with the turnaround.

So, in this case, a couple of options for the turnarounds are: If I make too much money, my spouse won't leave me, or if I make too much money, I may leave my spouse. (Note, the turnaround is very important and you want to turnaround the original question a couple of times like I demonstrated here.)

"The Work" is a very powerful way to help you see the truth of what's blocking you so you can work through those blocks.

So, now that we've covered what's blocking you internally from successfully marketing your business (and remember, if you need more help, definitely check out the Resources section), let's move to the external marketing strategies.

Part 2

YOUR OUTER GAME/MARKETING STRATEGIES

Chapter 4
EXTERNAL GAME: ONLINE MARKETING OVERVIEW

I was talking to a friend of mine after she had a disappointing launch.

She started off by telling me about all the soul-searching she had done after no one had bought. Then she shared with me what she thought the Universe was trying to tell her.

I listened quietly until she got to the radical business changes she was thinking about making based on this "message" from the Universe.

At that point I interrupted her.

"After your preview call," I said (a preview call is typically a free call where you teach some content and then make an offer), "how many emails did you send out to your list?"

Silence. Then:

"One, I guess."

"One? Which one did you send?"

"The recording email." (Basically the email providing the link to the recording of the preview call.)

I told her then I was pretty sure the only message the Universe was sending her was she didn't promote her program nearly enough.

The point is, there is a time and a place to work on the inner game of marketing and a time and place to work on the outer game. When you're in a middle of launching a new program, you definitely want to make sure you do everything you can from an external, outer game perspective to successfully promote and sell your program.

(For example, if you're serious about filling your new program, you're going to want to plan on sending more than one email promoting it.)

I also want to share that even seasoned entrepreneurs in the conscious entrepreneur space will confuse their marketing issues as being either an internal OR external block. In other words, it's not always easy to distinguish between the two. So, I'd like to invite you to work on both — do your inner work AND make sure you have all your ducks in a row and are following solid marketing practices. And when you do run into problems, don't assume to immediately know what the issue is. Instead, allow yourself to stay open to it being either an internal or external problem (or maybe both).

Okay, back to the external.

Let's talk about what it means to have solid, online marketing practices, beginning with a definition of online marketing.

Online marketing consists of:

- Strategies to find and attract your ideal prospects online.

- Strategies to begin — and nurture — a relationship with your ideal prospects (the bulk of these strategies being virtual).

- Strategies to inspire and invite them to become ideal clients (most of these strategies being virtual as well).

Sounds fairly straightforward, doesn't it? Okay, so now let's look at what each one of these categories entail.

- **Strategies to find and attract your ideal prospects online.** The Love Your Marketing Assessment in Chapter 5 will help you find and attract your ideal prospects online.

- **Strategies to begin — and nurture — a relationship with your ideal prospects.** Your website (which also includes any opt-in pages), free gift, and content/community is what helps you create and nurture a relationship with your ideal prospects. (We cover this in Chapter 6.)

- **Strategies to inspire and invite them to become ideal clients.** Sales letters, campaigns and product/program launches are what will help you inspire and invite your ideal prospects to become ideal clients. (We cover this in Chapter 7.)

So, in essence, you find your ideal prospects with the Love Your Marketing Assessment and invite them to deepen the relationship with you by visiting your website and/or downloading a free gift (you may want to send them directly to an opt-in page for the free gift).

In order for them to download your gift, they need to provide you with their contact information, so you're able to add them to your list (or your community).

You then can start to nurture a relationship with your ideal prospects by sending them content and/or interacting with them to help them feel like they know, like and trust you. Then, you can invite the ones who are ready to take things deeper to invest in a product or program or maybe some one-on-one work with you.

See how that all fits together?

Now, if you're new to the online marketing world, you may be feeling a bit confused by some of the terminology. No worries — I've included a glossary in the Appendix, so check that out at any time for additional clarity. The glossary may be helpful for you even if you're comfortable with Internet Marketing terms, but are interested in stepping more deeply into the love-based marketing world. After all, in order to make your marketing more love-based, you need to start with the vocabulary.

There's one last thing I want to cover before we move into the nitty-gritty of online marketing, and that's making sure you have three key foundational pieces in place — knowing who your ideal clients are, what your message is and what your mindset/"come from" is.

YOUR IDEAL CLIENTS

I cover ideal clients in great detail in my first Love-Based Copy book (Love-Based Copywriting Method) and your message in my second Love-Based Copy book (Love-Based Copywriting System), so all I'm going to do here is give you a few quick basics.

For me, I prefer the term "ideal clients" over something like "target market" or "niche," because to me, the phrases "target market" and "niche market" are both more external and demographic-based.

The term "ideal clients" is more focused on what's going on internally, including getting clear about their values, wants and desires. Ideal clients are ideal for you — they're your perfect clients — so not only do they love working with you, but you also love working with them. (No more dreading picking up the phone when it rings — you know what I'm talking about!)

> So, in a nutshell, by knowing who your ideal
> clients are, you know what makes them tick,
> and when you know that, you're more likely
> to effectively attract, inspire and invite them to
> work with you.

YOUR MESSAGE

For our purposes here, your message is the way you communicate what your business is about, what you offer, and how what you offer will solve the problem that's keeping your ideal clients up at night.

The more clarity you have around who your ideal clients are, and what your full message is, the easier it's going to be to craft and execute an Online Marketing Plan that actually will attract, inspire and invite your ideal clients into your business. This is why I consider those two pieces to be part of your foundation, because you actually build your Online Marketing Plan on top of them.

However, you don't have to have either of these foundational pieces perfectly in place in order to *start* getting yourself out there — to *start* attracting opportunities and paying clients. In fact, they might only be vague ideas when you begin, that you're sort of "throwing out there to see what sticks." (Which is perfectly okay — a big part of marketing is testing and tweaking.)

I definitely don't want you to use the fact you're not sure about your ideal client or message as a way to stop yourself — to keep yourself stuck in the "getting ready to get ready" phase. It's okay to go ahead and get started, no matter where you are in your business. (If you'd like some additional help with things like your ideal client and message, remember you can grab my other books, which I think would be a very smart move for you in this case. However, I ALSO don't want getting my other books to keep you from getting yourself out there!)

Just remember, it's not only possible but quite probable that you'll keep refining your ideal clients and message as you go, while you continue to market yourself.

Years ago, a friend of mine wanted to switch her ideal client group. She kept thinking her current clients and market weren't the ones she was supposed to be serving.

So, she did exactly that — she made the switch. And it was a total disaster. As it turned out, the new ideal client group wasn't ideal because they actually weren't online (and she wanted an online business — she was a coach and she was all about working at home and being able to find and serve her clients using the Internet).

Now, the point of this isn't to scare you off from trying something new. My friend was able to recover fairly quickly. But, had she never tried it, she would have constantly second-guessed herself about whether or not she was in the wrong market. (In fact, for about a good year before she actually made the switch, all she did was talk about it, so quite honestly, this was something she really needed to test.)

The "lesson": Don't be afraid to make a mistake. Instead, think of it as a way to test your beliefs and see if they're true or not.

There's a famous quote by Thomas Edison in which he responds to someone asking him about the ten thousand-some failures he had gone through while inventing the light bulb. His answer:

> "I don't have 10,000 failures. I know 10,000 ways a light bulb doesn't work."

A big part of your success as an entrepreneur is how quickly you recover from failure. Because failure IS going to happen — there's just no getting around it. So remember, it's about how quickly you can pick yourself up, dust yourself off and get back out there.

And to be clear, it's not uncommon to start your business off with one type of ideal client, and as you attract them to your business, realize they really aren't your ideal clients after all. But had you never attracted them in the first place, you wouldn't have known that. If my friend hadn't gone through what she did, she never would have realized how much of her lifestyle was built around her having an online business, and how she had to take that into consideration going forward with her business.

Sometimes knowing what you don't want is just as valuable as knowing what you do. And a lot of times, the only way you're going to know what you don't want is when you actually get it.

YOUR MINDSET/"COME FROM"

Let me ask you this:

When you approach your marketing, are you approaching it with a mindset of love and abundance, where you're attracting and inviting your perfect ideal clients in to your business? Are you okay with letting the less-than-perfect prospects go?

Or, are you approaching your marketing with a feeling of desperation, in dire need of clients, because you have bills to pay? Are you okay with attracting anyone who is able and willing to pay you, and are you afraid to let anyone go, even if you know in your heart he or she is not a good fit for you or your biz?

Remember, there's no judgment here. Every single business owner has been in the place where money is tight, where something isn't working, and where they really need their marketing to bring in some paying customers. (And they're okay if those clients aren't perfect, just as long as they pay.)

It happens. And it's nothing to be ashamed of.

The problem is, if you are feeling stressed or worried about money, it's going to be very difficult to use your marketing to educate people on their choices (in other words, hiring you or not), and to then stand back and allow them the space to make the best choice for them (which is what the Love-Based Copy and Online Marketing philosophy is all about).

When you're coming from desperation, you're much more likely to "twist arms," or pursue them more than you normally would in order to convince them to say "yes."

And you may do this even when coming from a good place. You know your product or service can help these prospects, and you just want to give them a little "push" to buy it. Sure, you need the money, but you know they'll get the transformation too, so it's a win-win.

Right?

Well ...

One of the things I talk about in my first two Love-Based Copy books is how I really don't believe in the whole "the ends justify the means" concept. To me, if you bring in clients using fear, shame, blame, guilt, anger or any sort of manipulation/fear-based emotion, you've brought that energy into the relationship. And because of that, they may always have a bit of a bad taste in their mouths (even if it's unconscious). They may also be more likely to drop out of your program, or disappear completely, or ask for a refund.

Now, if you're committed to not using fear-based emotions in your marketing, it will make things a lot easier if you take a few moments to shift your mindset into one of love and abundance before you sit down to work on any marketing tasks.

ACTION STEPS:

💜 Make a Conscious Choice — The very first thing you must do if you haven't already is to make a conscious choice one way or another: to use fear-based marketing OR to use love-based marketing.

If you choose love, then it's important to take a few moments and make sure your mindset is on board with your choice — and this is especially true before you start any actual marketing activities.

💜 Complete One or All of the Activities in the Appendix — Begin making mindset shifts.

💜 If You'd Like Additional Help — Watch for the release of my Love-Based Money and Mindset book this year.

💜 Download Your Love-Based Online Marketing Workbook — If you haven't already, now is a great time to do so. It's designed to help guide you through the strategies laid out in the upcoming chapters to make it easier for you to craft your Online Marketing Plan. You can download it here: www.lovebasedonlinemaketing.com/workbook

Chapter 5
FINDING AND ATTRACTING IDEAL PROSPECTS

One of my friends, Jeanna Gabellini, a Law of Attraction and Abundance Expert, once told me that she believes marketing can get be one of *the* most creative activities we do as entrepreneurs. Yet so often we resist … both marketing in general, AND being creative with our marketing.

Maybe we resist because we think we hate marketing or we think we aren't good at it or we feel like it's loaded with "shoulds" (i.e. I really should be marketing).

Or maybe we resist because we take it way too seriously — if we're struggling with cash flow in our business, suddenly marketing can feel critical — like life or death to our business — and it's difficult to find any sort of fun in something so full of pressure.

(And don't even get me started about how we resist our creativity — that's definitely another book for another time.)

So, this chapter is all about helping you relax when it comes to your marketing (and maybe, just maybe … you'll even have some fun with it!).

It all starts with turning around how you think about marketing.

One of the reasons why you may think you hate marketing could be because you don't like the actual activity you think you need to be doing to market yourself.

For instance, if you hate writing, and you feel that writing articles on a blog is the best way to market yourself, then you're probably going to hate marketing.

However, there's a little-known secret about marking — there are A LOT of marketing tactics out there. And I would bet that there is AT LEAST one marketing activity that you at least enjoy, if not love.

(And remember, part of Love-Based Online Marketing philosophy is to love your marketing!)

So, how do you know which marketing tactic (what I call your Marketing Love Factor) is right for you? I'm so glad you asked …

It's time to take my Love Your Marketing Assessment, below, to help you figure it out. Enjoy!

LOVE YOUR MARKETING ASSESSMENT

Directions: read each statement and rank how strongly you resonate — or don't resonate — with each statement.

1. You love providing laser coaching or working one-on-one with clients to get to the heart of their challenges.

1	3	5
Don't resonate at all	Neutral	Strongly resonate with

2. You love speaking in front of big groups.

1	3	5
Don't resonate at all	Neutral	Strongly resonate with

3. You love speaking in front of small groups.

1	3	5
Don't resonate at all	Neutral	Strongly resonate with

4. You love being interviewed virtually.

1	3	5
Don't resonate at all	Neutral	Strongly resonate with

5. You love speaking, but you're not crazy about standing in front of live groups — you prefer speaking via telephone or webinar.

1	3	5
Don't resonate at all	Neutral	Strongly resonate with

6. You love interviewing people — hosting other people's content.

1	3	5
Don't resonate at all	Neutral	Strongly resonate with

7. You love writing books or other long pieces of work.

1	3	5
Don't resonate at all	Neutral	Strongly resonate with

8. You love writing shorter, snappier pieces (300-700 words).

1	3	5
Don't resonate at all	Neutral	Strongly resonate with

9. You love being on television.

1	3	5
Don't resonate at all	Neutral	Strongly resonate with

10. You love being on video.

1	3	5
Don't resonate at all	Neutral	Strongly resonate with

11. You love connecting with people online.

1	3	5
Don't resonate at all	Neutral	Strongly resonate with

12. You love commenting and responding to what other people say online.

1	3	5
Don't resonate at all	Neutral	Strongly resonate with

13. You love real-time online chatting.

1	3	5
Don't resonate at all	Neutral	Strongly resonate with

14. You love working with the media and creating a buzz on media outlets.

1	3	5
Don't resonate at all	Neutral	Strongly resonate with

15. You love in-person networking.

1	3	5
Don't resonate at all	Neutral	Strongly resonate with

16. You love building websites and testing and tweaking elements such as headlines.

1	3	5
Don't resonate at all	Neutral	Strongly resonate with

17. You love writing sales copy (copywriting) — emails, sales letters, etc.

1	3	5
Don't resonate at all	Neutral	Strongly resonate with

SCORING:

Now, review your answers, and write down the ones you most resonated with (in other words, write down your 5's). Note: We've provided space for this in the the companion Workbook.

Then, use the key below to identify a specific marketing strategy that aligns with each statement.

Statement 1 — Live Q&A or coaching calls or maybe a "makeover" radio show

Statement 2 — Speaking on big stages

Statement 3 — Speaking in front of small, intimate groups

Statement 4 — Being interviewed by other people — either on radio shows or podcasts

Statement 5 — Speaking in teleclasses

Statement 6 — Hosting your own radio show or podcast

Statement 7 — Writing books

Statement 8 — Writing articles or blog posts

Statement 9 — Hosting a television show

Statement 10 — Video

Statement 11 — Social networking

Statement 12 — Social networking with an emphasis on commenting on blogs and online groups

Statement 13 — Twitter

Statement 14 — Publicity or public relations

Statement 15 — Networking groups

Statements 16 and 17 — Internet Marketing (or just Marketing in general). This includes tactics like Facebook ads. (If this is you — and you're someone who really doesn't like interacting with people much, you may really enjoy marketing through paid online ads.)

And there you have it!

If you have a clear favorite — hooray! That's your Marketing Love Factor!

If you have a tie (for instance, you enjoy speaking in person in front of big and small groups equally), sit with it for a bit. It may mean you have 2 Marketing Love Factors, but I suspect you have one favorite and one that's a close second.

If you do have a tie (or multiple ties), don't rush the process. Ask your Inner Wisdom or your intuition for help — one of them is your MOST favorite and the one you're MOST suited for — but that doesn't mean you don't have multiple talents and it also doesn't mean you can't capitalize on them when you create your Online Marketing Plan.

In addition, make a list of those that are your least favorite, or that you resonate least with. Those are the ones you'll want to hire a team to help you implement. Yes, they are important to your marketing plan, but you certainly don't need to do them yourself.

Typically what you want to do is start with one marketing tactic, in this case, your Marketing Love Factor, and make that the centerpiece of your marketing activities. Once that's working for you and bringing in a steady source of ideal prospects, then you can start adding other marketing tactics (and if you're adding tactics that you don't particularly enjoy, then you can start bringing in team members as well).

In Chapter 9, I'll show you how to build your Online Marketing Plan around your Marketing Love Factor.

Now that you know which marketing activity is best suited to your preferences when it comes to finding and attracting your ideal prospects, let's talk about how you can then start building and nurturing your list/community.

Chapter 6
BUILDING AND NURTURING YOUR LIST/ COMMUNITY

Once you've attracted your ideal prospects, the next step is to get them to raise their hand and give you permission to contact them. By doing so, they're basically allowing you to start a relationship with them, so they can get to know you. (And people tend to buy from those they know, like and trust.)

The way you want to get their permission online is to have them give you their contact information — in most cases their name and email. That's how you build your list/community. (Remember, I would much rather you think about your list of prospects as your community versus your list — I realize it IS a list and I also realize it's common jargon in the Internet Marketing world to call it a "list" — but list is a bit dehumanizing. That's why I like "community" or "list/community" better, because it helps remind us there are living, breathing humans on the other end of that email address. And the more we remember that, the easier it is to embrace the Love-Based Copy and Marketing philosophy.)

Nurturing your list/community takes place when you actually communicate with your ideal prospects. So, every time you're sending content or promotional materials, you're in effect nurturing the relationship.

BUILDING YOUR COMMUNITY

Typically, what you'll want to do to build your community is to send your ideal prospects to a page — like your website, or an opt-in page. (Opt-in pages are those pages that ask you to input your name and email address in exchange for a free gift — maybe a book or resource, or access to a webinar or training of some kind).

For this strategy to work, you need to create:

- Some sort of gift or freebie to give to your ideal prospects.

- A website page or opt-in page (or both).

- A thank you page and autoresponder to deliver the gift.

Let's start with the gift itself.

Usually, the gift is some sort of downloadable, valuable information, such as:

- Something written — an eBook, special report, checklist, blueprint, template, etc. It could also be a quiz or an assessment people take and then need to opt in to in order receive the results, or even a training delivered via email.

- An audio — a recording of content, a meditation, a guided exercise … you get the idea.

- A video or video series — any type of video training.

The point of this gift is to give your ideal clients a taste of your offerings, so they get a taste of you: a taste of your teachings or expertise, and a taste of what they can expect if they decide to work with you. (As my good friend Wealthy Thought Leader Andrea J. Lee likes to say — this is your "pink spoon." Remember how Baskin Robbins would give you a "pink spoon" taste of the different flavors of ice cream so you could choose the one you like best before you buy? This is the same concept; you're giving your tribe a "pink spoon" taste of the transformation you offer.)

Now, it should be designed around something specific that keeps your ideal prospects up at night, to ensure they will find it valuable enough to give you their information in the first place.

Typically the best free gifts for opt ins look like this:

- You address an immediate need your ideal prospects have. It's likely around some sort of pain they're in — something that keeps them up at night. (One quick, important note here: If the thought of talking about your ideal client's pain bothers you because you don't think it's love-based, I promise you, that couldn't be further from the truth. For more on why avoiding talking about your ideal prospect's pain is actually a huge disservice, to you and him or her, definitely check out either of my first two Love-Based Copy books.)

- 💜 Your answer (which should be in the form of some sort of content) addresses that pain and offers a solution, but it then opens up a second problem (or gap) that working with you in one of your paid programs would address.

Here's an example of how this would work:

Let's say one of your core programs helps women heal their thyroid gland naturally, so they don't need prescription medication.

For your free gift, you could design a self-assessment that helps women self-diagnose potential thyroid issues. If, from that self-assessment, they do discover a problem, then your course is the obvious next step.

Or, your freebie could be a list of the top 10 foods that help women heal their thyroid naturally, and the top 5 foods to avoid. That's a great start to getting better, right?

But if the woman wants to go deeper and fully heal her thyroid, because while changing her diet is a good start, it's only the beginning of the full healing process — she'll need to enroll in your program.

So, in other words, your freebie is the perfect introduction to your core message and business offerings. You'll know that the people who opt in are already interested in what you sell, because your freebie is an extension of what you sell. You're not, for example, offering free recipes and then selling a course on how to make money using Facebook ads.

It's important to keep in mind that you're probably going to need to create a number of different freebies throughout the course of your business. You'll likely need one general gift you offer on your website, another that is specific for interviews you do, another for programs you're a part of, and still others that will become part of your launches of your products or programs.

In addition, your freebie will likely also change over the years as your business grows and matures. As you continuously develop clarity about your ideal clients and their needs, you also tweak and clarify your message, or shift it entirely, to fit them.

I'm telling you this so you don't get stuck in the "has to be perfect" phase, which of course will keep you stuck in general. Don't be afraid to just get something up on your site. It absolutely does NOT need to be perfect. It won't be the last freebie you create for your business, and you can always tweak it and improve it … it's important to just start somewhere. (Remember what I said in the last chapter about not being afraid to make mistakes.)

HOW TO OFFER YOUR FREEBIE

Okay, so once you have your freebie created, then you need to get it up on a web page or an opt-in page.

In order to do that, you'll need:

- A url (you definitely need to own a distinct url as an entrepreneur, and much like freebies, you'll probably end up owning lots of them). You can purchase urls at places like GoDaddy.com.

- Hosting of your url (if you don't know where to start with a web host, you can check with the place you bought your url from — many of them offer web hosting).

- Either an HTML editor or a program such as Wordpress to create the actual website pages. (Wordpress is based on a blogging platform and is easier than HTML to create your own website or opt-in pages.) You may need some technical help to get things set up initially, but especially if you end up using something like Wordpress, you can likely build your website from there and make your own changes. (Note: Don't go to Wordpress and open an account there, because then the url will be hosted on the Wordpress site and it won't be your own. You need to have Wordpress uploaded on your site. A technical person can help you get this set up if you have questions, or if this just isn't your cup of tea.)

- 💜 An email program to collect emails and that also allows you to email your list. Programs like Constant Contact, Mail Chimp or Aweber are commonly used by many entrepreneurs. Again, you may want to have a technical person help you get all of this set up, and then you can choose to take it over yourself, or have them continue to support you. (Note: My company also has a technical division if you'd like us to help you get set up — see the Resources section for more details.)

- 💜 The copy for the opt-in pages, thank you page, and autoresponder. (My "Love-Based Copy System" is the perfect book to walk you through writing your own copy, if that's something you feel like you need help with.)

Once you have all of these pieces in place, you use your Marketing Love Factor to get that url in front of your ideal clients. It doesn't matter what your MLF (Marketing Love Factor) really is; whatever it is that you're doing to promote yourself and your business, you always end with a call to action that provides prospects with more information. You let them know they can visit your site and download your gift, which of course means they then become a part of your list/community, and you have permission to reach out and contact them again. More on this in Chapter 9 when you create your Online Marketing Plan.)

Now, once your ideal prospects are opting in and you're gathering their contact information, it's time to start building a relationship with them. And the way you do that is by sending them content.

You can create your content via audio, video or written word. Then, you email your community with that content (or a link so they can go download or view the content somewhere else, for instance on a blog).

You could also create an ezine or email newsletter to send to your community, which nurtures your relationship with your followers even more, because it's another way you get to "touch" them.

Now, when I talk about creating content, I'm not talking about writing a book every week. You can keep it short — maybe a few quick tips, or a short, one-minute video, or even an email that provides your answers to your community's top questions. (Bonus tip: If you end up crafting a podcast, you can then share other people's content or expertise by interviewing them, too, so you're also nurturing your list with other people's content.)

Basically, what you want to do is share your expertise with your community in bite-sized pieces.

(And no, you don't have to do all the creating yourself. You certainly can use a ghost writer to help you craft your content.)

Now, how often should you email content to your community? I would say either once a week or once every other week, minimally.

In addition to sending your community content, you also want to provide additional ways for them to get to know you. You can do that by sharing your personality, things that are happening in your life right now, your vulnerabilities, details about your family, your kids, your pets, your vacations, etc. It's often a good idea to share something personal in your content emails, before you get into the content itself.

Of course, creating and nurturing your community is all well and good, but as a business owner, you also need a way to turn your ideal prospects into ideal clients. That's what we'll focus on in the next chapter.

Chapter 7
INVITING YOUR IDEAL PROSPECTS TO BECOME IDEAL CLIENTS

It's time to talk about how to inspire and invite your ideal prospects to say "yes!" to working more closely with you, by becoming actual, paying ideal clients.

There are a number of directions you can go with this, and part of what I want to accomplish in this chapter is to give you some guidance on choosing the right direction for you.

There are also a couple of things to keep in mind here. First off, *the direction you may have the most success with and the direction that's right for you may not be the same direction*.

What do I mean by that? Well, for instance, when you're first starting out, the fastest, easiest way to start making money and building a business is to work with clients one-on-one. But, working with clients one-on-one may NOT be what you're best suited for.

If that's the case, what do you do? Well, you have a couple of options.

1.   You can begin by working with clients one-on-one in order to generate cash flow and visibility for yourself, while *at the same time* working to get the necessary

91

pieces in place to make money in other ways that don't require one-on-one time.

OR

2. You can immediately launch your business without selling your time, knowing you're probably not going to make enough money to sustain yourself for a while (which means if you choose this route, you probably need to have another income source while you build your business).

You also may not know which business model is best for you right now — OR, you may be convinced you're supposed to work with people in large groups, but you actually prefer working closely with a small handful of folks, or even one-on-one.

All of this is perfectly okay — sometimes, the only way you can learn what you really do want is by doing what you don't want.

The most important thing is to start.

That brings us to my next main point, which is how to sell what your business is offering.

BEST STRATEGIES FOR SELLING WHAT YOUR BUSINESS OFFERS

Services (especially one-on-one) — Whether we're talking about some sort of coaching or consulting (including VIP days — when you spend the day with a client to really dig deep into whatever challenge he or she is dealing with) or done-for-you services, the easiest way to sell these services is with a one-on-one sales call. Either you, the entrepreneur, get on the phone with the prospective client yourself, or you have someone from your sales team get on the phone with the prospective client.

There are a couple of reasons why it's easiest to sell services via a sales call, as opposed to a launch, or just having them visit a sales page on your site. First, this is typically a higher-priced sale, which typically means your prospect will have more questions. Also, prospective clients want to make sure your offer is a good fit for them, and getting on the phone with someone from your team is a great way to determine that.

Of course, in order to sell your services via a sales call, you need to get people on the phone. (This is also why offering a free gift in exchange for contact information plus permission to reach out to your ideal prospects is so important, because once you have that, you can offer an opportunity for them to speak with you or someone on your team .)

The easiest way to get people on the phone with you is to send an email or a series of emails that either offer a straight sales call (letting people know in the copy what you offer and how that offer will help solve their specific problems — and if they'd like to know more, they are invited to set up a free call with you). Or, you can offer something called a free strategy or discovery session.

If you're a coach offering a coaching package, you're probably going to want to offer a strategy session. Strategy sessions are free, but to be totally clear, they are NOT free coaching sessions. Instead, they're opportunities to explore whether or not the two of you are a good fit to work together.

During this strategy session, you basically help your ideal prospect discover his or her biggest problem — what's keeping him or her awake at night — in order to see if your services or program is a good fit to help him or her eliminate it.

You can use strategy sessions to not only sell one-on-one services, coaching and VIP days, but pretty much any sort of program that costs more than $2,000.

Whether you're setting up straight sales calls or free strategy sessions, you may want to look into automating the process of inviting people to get on the phone with you. One way to do that is to set up an autoresponder series (also known as an AR series). AR series are emails that are sent out automatically — you write them in advance, program them into an email program such as Aweber or 1Shopping Cart, and the program sends them out automatically for you.

Here's how this would work:

A prospect opts in to your email list. Over the course of the next week, he is then sent a series of 5 emails that provide some content and that also offer the opportunity to sign up for a free strategy session.

Typically, the first autoresponder provides the actual freebie, and then the next one or two emails provide some free, valuable content that makes sense with the freebie. Then, the last two or three emails cover the offer — a sales call or a free strategy session.

Products or Programs (this includes information products, physical products such as shoes, group programs, events, books, etc.). If the price of the product or program is under $2,000, then it's very possible to sell it directly online through some sort of launch or sale. If the price is over $2,000, you'll likely want to look at selling via a strategy session or sales call, so you'll probably want to set up a campaign similar to how you would sell services (see previous section in this chapter).

Now, before I get into the different ways to sell products online, I want to explain why it's easier to sell one-on-one services and start creating cash flow when you're first starting out (i.e. when you don't have much of a list or a community) a bit more.

Obviously, once you have a list/community, it becomes easier to sell products and programs because you have the following to whom you can get your products and programs in front of on a fairly regular basis.

But keep in mind, you'll need to sell an awful lot of products or programs to completely replace one-on-one services.

One of the reasons it's more difficult selling products and programs when you have a small community is because of conversions. Let me explain.

CONVERSIONS

When we're talking one-on-one sales calls, it's not unheard of to get 1-2 new clients for every 5 prospects you talk to — especially if you are only talking to warm leads who have taken the initiative to set up a call with you (which is what the above autoresponder campaign encourages). In addition, it's possible to get these sort of conversions when you're asking people to buy a more expensive program or service (i.e. $2,000 and up). You obviously need fewer clients than if you were selling let's say a $100 product.

It's also quite possible to have an even higher conversion. When I was a freelancer, I probably ended up with 8 new clients for every 10 I talked to (they were pretty warm by the time they got to me — they already knew they wanted to hire a copywriter, so by the time I was speaking with them, it was mainly just to see if working with me was the right fit for them).

Compare that conversion (8 out of 10) to online sales — generally speaking, if you get 1% conversion (which is 1 person buying out of 100 who look at the sales page), you're doing really well.

On top of that, you also need to take into consideration how, if you have a list of let's say 100 people, you can safely assume that not all 100 are going to go look at your sales page. Depending on the relationship you have with your list (and, quite honestly, you'll probably have a closer relationship when you only have 100 people on it versus 1,000 or 10,000), you could expect anywhere from 5% to 30% clicking through to the actual sales page.

Now, you can increase the number of people who are looking at your sales page and also increase how many actually buy if you do a launch or a sale (more about both of those below) and by using both of those tactics, entrepreneurs are able to make a living selling info-products. But, it's still going to be a lower conversion than getting on the phone with your ideal prospects.

Bottom line — if you want to make a living simply selling products and programs to your list and community, you are likely going to need a minimum of 10,000 folks in your community.

(Now, a quick note on numbers — 10,000 is actually on the low side for most people, but it truly depends on the relationship you have with your list. I do know some entrepreneurs who had smaller lists and were able to generate over 6 figures in products and programs sales. But others I know needed a list and community of 50,000 to accomplish the same thing. These are just ballpark numbers to give you some idea about how to best package your offerings, depending on where you currently are in your business. This also lets you know what you probably need to shoot for, if you want to change your business model.)

In addition, remember that I'm talking ONLY about selling straight products and programs to your list here — I'm not talking about selling a combination of one-on-one services with products. I know a lot of folks who broke 6 figures with list/communities that were a little over 1,000, and who were making multiple 6 figures or even 7 figures with a list/community of under 10,000. BUT they were selling a combination of products, programs and one-on-one services. So if you're willing to sell both, you open up even more opportunity for yourself.

Okay, now that you have some background information on conversions and numbers when selling products, let's dive in and take a look at different types of launches. This way, you can determine which is right for you, based on your specific situation and ultimate goal.

TYPES OF LAUNCHES

Product Launch Formula — Made famous by Jeff Walker, this is a specific time-based launch driving to an open enrollment period for your program, where you "open the cart" (give people the option to buy) for a few days and then "close the cart" (or close enrollment). The "cart" refers to the shopping cart — so you're opening and closing the shopping cart, which effectively determines when a person can buy.

During the pre-launch phase — this is when the cart is not officially open yet, but the launch has started — you give away a bunch of free content, much of it video-based. The content seeds the actual program, so when you open the cart, you've already created demand for the program. The entire promotional period is basically an event, in and of itself.

A typical PLF (stands for Product Launch Formula) usually looks something like this:

- 3 pieces of free content are released — typically a combination of video training and download (a book, a checklist, etc.). The videos tend to be over 20 minutes (usually 30-40 minutes total).

- This leads to some sort of event when you officially open the cart — a lot of folks choose to host a webinar, but you can also do a livestream or create another video.

- You may also have a different event to close the cart (maybe some sort of Q&A or hot seat coaching call).

As you can see, these launches are generally a lot of work, with many moving pieces. It really doesn't make sense to do all of this work unless you're selling a product that is between $1000 (or $997) and $2,000 (or $1997), to make sure you get a healthy ROI.

(For products less than $1000, you would likely do a much simpler launch, perhaps with just one freebie and one webinar — or even just a single webinar. See next section.)

Now, let's go back to conversions for a moment. In order for a traditional product launch to work, you need a lot of people to consume the pre-launch material, which means you either need to spend money in paid advertising, or line up joint venture partners or affiliates to promote your pre-launch material to their lists and communities.

A joint venture partner (JV) or affiliate is an entrepreneur who promotes other entrepreneur's product launches for a commission — typically about 40% of the cost of the product. (You only pay them when they make a sale for you.)

On the surface, this sounds like a great deal, right? People promote you for free, and you only pay them if someone on their list actually purchases something. (You know if they make a sale for you because you give your joint venture or affiliate partners a unique tracking link, and they send out emails or post on social media using that link. The shopping cart then tracks that link — so you'll know where your sales come from.)

Alas, like most "too good to be true" scenarios, dig a little deeper and it doesn't look quite so rosy.

There is no question that affiliates and joint venture partners are promoting you in order to get a commission. But, they are also promoting you because they want you to promote them. So, if you have little to no list, it's going to be very difficult to land a big joint venture partner, because those big joint venture partners are going to want to play with other entrepreneurs who have a similar big list.

Also, the arrangement puts a lot of pressure on you to make sure you actually convert prospects for your partner, as well. In other words, if a big joint venture partner promotes you, and then you don't actually convert any sales for her, chances are high that she's going to be far less likely to promote you in the future.

Now, if you're just starting out and have little to no list, does that mean you can't do a product launch? Absolutely not — first off, you can definitely still find people to promote you, but you're going to have to look for people who also have smaller lists. That's a start, though, and it's how you grow. You can also look at paid advertising, and organic posting on social media to get the ball rolling.

A note about paid advertising: it can seem like a drag at first, can't it? You have to pay no matter what the outcome is — regardless of how many new clients it brings in. The benefits: you don't have to promote anyone in return. (And, quite honestly, if you line up too many folks to reciprocate promotions with, you can very quickly end up burning out your list by promoting too much and too often, so there is definitely a drawback to too much promoting, as well.) You also won't have to worry about hard feelings, if the launch doesn't go as planned. Facebook will still happily take your money for your next launch, even if one bombs. ;)

Other Types of Product Launches — This next model is a modified or "scaled down" product launch from the Jeff Walker model above, and it's a great option if you don't feel like messing around with long videos and JVs, or if the product you're selling is less than $997. (Again, while it IS possible to do a full product launch for a product less than $997, unless you have an awfully big reach, the return on your money, time and energy investment isn't really there.)

A popular way to scale down the Product Launch Formula is to simply skip the 3 pieces of pre-launch content you'd offer initially, and ONLY offer either a webinar or teleseminar that sells your program. (Teleseminars are phone only — you get a bridge line and people listen either online or on the phone, and you deliver some content and make an offer; a webinar includes slides your participants can view, so you typically need to watch it online either on a computer or a tablet, or on a mobile phone.)

These are much simpler to set up — all you need to do is put up one opt-in page where people can sign up to attend the training, send out a few emails and/or promote on social networking, deliver the call or webinar, and sell the program.

The downside is you likely will sell less than you would with the full PLF because each piece of pre-launch content is designed to really hook your ideal prospects — you give them valuable content, and by the time they've consumed all of it, they can't wait to work with you. (However, if you're just starting out and have no list, or a small list, you're not going to sell a lot no matter which launch formula you use, so it probably makes more sense to do the modified version.)

Now, there's something else to keep in mind with product launches, and this is important — they're not really designed for you to keep doing them over and over. In other words, if you do a launch one month and you don't make your financial goals, trying to do another launch right away the following month likely isn't going to work either.

This is one of the reasons why people DO the whole PLF — because, if done right, you can make quite a bit of money in one month (multiple 6 figures or even 7 figures) which will then carry you over until your next launch (which in many cases is 6 months or a year later).

This is another reason why it's difficult to build a business selling products and group programs when you're first starting out, so having regular income from one-to-one clients can really help. (Also, it's not uncommon for product launches to simultaneously boost your one-on-one client work — so along with making you money, product launches also are a fabulous way to bump up your visibility, credibility and marketing momentum.)

Now, there IS one type of launch that's designed to constantly bring new clients into your business, without much work from you. It's called the Evergreen Launch.

Evergreen Launch — The idea around this type of launch is that it's completely automated. All you need to do is send prospects to opt in to the launch sequence to see sales come in. In many cases, this is a webinar driven launch — you invite new prospects to opt in for a webinar, which automatically plays at specific times and dates you set in advance (for instance, you can set it so every Wednesday at 1 pm, the webinar automatically plays). The email reminders are all automated, as is the follow-up sequence, which typically includes emails that drive to an encore presentation at another set time in case they missed it, and then emails that drive directly to a sales page.

So again, *everything is automated*, including the process of receiving payment when folks purchase.

Sounds like the Internet Marketing dream come true, eh? You truly make money in your sleep!

Except ... well, like so many other things in life, this is just not as easy as it may seem.

First of all, in order for this to work, you need an actual, proven, effective sales campaign. This means you need to have created a webinar that actually converts (makes sales), and your emails need to actually work to get people to the webinar (along with successfully directing them to the sales page after). So, if you've never done any of this before, the chances of you creating a winning campaign the first time out are pretty slim.

In fact, most of my entrepreneurial friends and clients who are making money this way have spent hours tweaking and testing the webinar (and they've usually had either professional copywriters write their materials for them, like my company, or they've spent *hours* working on the copy themselves) to make sure everything will convert the way they want before ever loading it up into all the automated platforms.

Also, you should be aware that conversions are always lower for evergreen launches than live launches. In other words, if you create a live launch that converts like crazy, you should know your evergreen conversions are not going to be nearly as high. (Which doesn't mean it won't be successful and profitable overall, it's just something to be aware of. I suspect the numbers are generally lower because the evergreen launch lacks the excitement and "presence" of a live launch: think social media, affiliate partner mailings, generating a buzz through speaking, etc.)

It's also not quite as automated as you think, because it's not exactly a "set and forget" type strategy. You need to keep "feeding the beast," as they say. In other words, you need to *constantly* send prospects to the opt-in page to get this to work. So, you either need to be out there hustling joint venture and affiliate partners to promote your evergreen launch for you, or you need to be spending money on advertising (such as Facebook ads) — or, you need to be doing both, simultaneously.

ADVERTISING

Now, I've already covered joint venture and affiliate partners, so here, I'd like to cover a few more things to consider when it comes to advertising, other than the obvious: you could end up paying an awful lot of money to say, Facebook (for advertising) before you ever start seeing a profit.

Yes, once you have your online/Facebook ad dialed in, you're as close to a "set and forget" campaign as you could possibly be, since all you really need to do at that point is make sure you're paying the credit card bill to keep the ad online.

But in reality, you have to keep an eye on it. Ads do get old, and they can stop converting online, so they need to be monitored, tweaked, and occasionally replaced.

All that said, once you DO get an evergreen launch working, it can be a super-fabulous way to make consistent cash, with new ideal clients flowing into your business each and every month. But, for the most part, it isn't a great strategy for a beginning business.

To me, this is a more advanced business and marketing strategy. Even when you have a proven webinar and email string, it's not cheap to set up — it will take significant resources — both time and money. Plus, when you're a beginner, you may not have mastered the high-conversion webinar yet. So, if this launch format sounds good to you, I suggest building up to it: start by creating a few small webinar launches and see how they go. If you have great conversions, you can then start tweaking them into an evergreen process.

If you're looking for something that can happen all the time, along with the Evergreen Product Launch, there is one other campaign you can set up for consistent cash flow.

Setting up Your Product as Part of an Autoresponder Series
— This is similar to how you would set up an AR series if you were selling services or strategy sessions, except instead of offering a call with you or your sales team in your email correspondence, you offer a product.

Now, if you do this, it needs to be an inexpensive product. I would say the cheaper the better — definitely under $100 and maybe even under $50. Remember, these are folks who have just joined your list and community, so they're still getting to know you and they probably aren't going to be open to a big investment without a lot more work on your part (like inviting them into a webinar, similar to the evergreen strategy above).

The easiest way to do this is to give them some sort of sale or one-time offer. Either they get the offer right away on the thank you page after they opt in, or you present it to them after 2-3 content emails, while providing them with some sort of coupon code. You want to send them directly to a sales page so they can read more and (hopefully) purchase right there, from the page.

The downside is, just like the Evergreen Launch Model, you need a consistent lead source. In this case, you could use either paid ads or more organic traffic sources such as blog posts, videos or podcasts. (Keep in mind while the organic sounds a lot better since it's, well, free, it typically takes some time to get it up and running. The big advantage of paid advertising is that it's immediate — you'll start to see immediate results for your efforts.)

Having a Sale. This last type of "launch" really isn't a launch, but it IS still an event that can bring in money, so I'm including it here. (I talk more about sales, and provide you with a worksheet to figure out the details of your specific sale in my "Holiday Marketing Secrets" special report — see Resource section.)

In a nutshell, if you decide to have a sale, you definitely need a reason (although there are lots of reasons out there, such as having a sale around your birthday or a holiday). And the way to set it up is to send 3-4 emails within a short span of time, no longer than a week, offering that sale.

Now, sales, like launches, can't be done all the time, so again, you need to make sure you still have cash flow coming in on the months when you aren't hosting a sale.

> 💜 Important: If a sale or launch doesn't go as planned, don't panic. Maybe offer VIP days or a different type of

offer right after — either higher end or lower end (an upsell OR downsell) to see what happens. You can also support other people's launches as an affiliate and make money that way. At the very least, take comfort knowing you've created momentum in your business.

***

In Chapter 9, when I walk you through creating your Online Marketing Plan, I'll talk about how you can customize all these strategies specifically for yourself and your biz, but first, I want to talk about a very important — but often overlooked — foundational marketing piece.

Part 3

CRAFT YOUR ONLINE MARKETING PLAN

Chapter 8
LONG-TERM AND SHORT-TERM MARKETING STRATEGIES

To be successful in business, you need to implement both long-term and short-term marketing strategies.

The problem is, many entrepreneurs and business owners don't know what constitutes a long-term or a short-term marketing strategy. And, by not knowing the difference, you could be hampering your business' growth, as well as putting unnecessary financial strain on yourself and your business.

Long-term strategies don't yield a quick return on your investment but are instead designed to grow your business and stabilize your cash flow; short-term strategies are designed to get cash in the door immediately.

So you see, if you use a long-term strategy when you should be using a short-term (or vice versa), you're not going to get the results you're looking for. Implementing a long-term marketing strategy when you need cash now could end up with you may end up going bankrupt before you can actually convert that long-term marketing strategy into cash.

Plus, when entrepreneurs are short on cash, they often start marketing to get themselves out of that situation. In and of itself, that's perfectly acceptable … *as long as the marketing strategy they choose is designed to bring in money in the short term AND*

is in alignment with how they've chosen to market their business.
(In other words, if they are striving to be a love-based business, then even when they're short on cash, they should continue to market in a love-based manner. It's seductive to switch to fear-based tactics in these situations — but that's the worst thing you can do. Not because fear doesn't sometimes work, but because switching back and forth between love and fear can cause confusion in the marketplace and end up backfiring on the entrepreneur.)

You may be wondering why you would ever choose a long-term marketing strategy, if it means you have to wait to see the results. Well, long-term marketing strategies tend to add stability to your income and your business over time. They're designed to help you grow your business — whereas short-term marketing strategies rarely result in consistent, long-term growth.

Now let's jump into the specifics around long- and short-term marketing strategies.

COMMON LONG-TERM MARKETING STRATEGIES

- 💜 List building (That's right — building your list is a long-term strategy — while building your list can also result in short-term sales, especially if you have an autoresponder series set up that leads new subscribers to one of your products or services, many times getting on your list and into your community is simply the first step in the process of the new subscriber getting to know you — to see if your message and expertise is right for him/her.)

💜 Public relations

💜 Sending an ezine or regular content to your list

💜 Blogging

💜 Posting content videos

💜 Podcasting

💜 Building and nurturing relationships on social networking platforms

💜 Speaking (especially if you don't make an offer or it's a low investment offer)

💜 SEO (search engine optimization)

💜 Writing a book

💜 Branding activities

As you can see, pretty much any activity that builds your expertise, visibility and credibility is, for the most part, a long-term strategy. Also, I mentioned this under the list-building notes but it bears repeating — just because it's a long-term strategy doesn't mean you can't make a sale from it. It's just not the focus of the strategy (and if you try to make it the focus, it tends to backfire).

COMMON SHORT-TERM MARKETING STRATEGIES

- 💜 Any type of product launch or sale to your list/community

- 💜 An offer for a strategy session or sales call

- 💜 Speaking — but ONLY if you're able to make an offer (minimally, a $500 offer — I recommend a price point of $1000 or higher)

- 💜 Picking up the phone and asking for referrals or sales. (Note — if you need clients, this is the fastest way to get them. And yes, I know this is more of a sales strategy than a marketing strategy, but regardless, it's a solid strategy that can help you get money in the door.)

As you can see, short-term marketing strategies tend to focus around making an offer.

Now, you can probably see why you need both long-term and short-term marketing strategies. Long-term strategies are about attracting your ideal tribe and connecting with them. Short-term strategies are about inviting them to take action and become a client or customer.

Here's another way to look at this: People buy from people they know, like and trust. Long-term marketing strategies focus on the know, like and trust aspects. Short-term marketing strategies focus on getting the sale. But regardless of which marketing strategy you're focusing on — long-term or short-term — it's important to stay in alignment with whatever you've chosen as the foundation for your business and your marketing, whether that's love-based or fear-based.

Up next — it's time to pull it all together and create your Online Marketing Plan!

Chapter 9
CREATING YOUR ONLINE MARKETING PLAN

This is it — where the rubber meets the road!

Let's create your Online Marketing Plan. (Yay!)

Having an Online Marketing Plan is one of the first steps to take when you want to start building a business you love, and that loves you back. After all, when you have a destination in mind, you really need a map to get you there, don't you? Otherwise, who knows where you'll end up!

Now, obviously this plan won't do much of anything at all for you, if you don't actually implement it. I'll talk more about that later. First thing's first …

If you haven't already taken the Love Your Marketing Assessment in Chapter 5, now is the time! Your Marketing Love Factor really is the foundation of your Online Marketing Plan. So if you don't identify it, it's going to be more difficult to fill out your plan.

In addition, this is also a great time to grab your Love-Based Online Marketing Workbook, too, as it's designed to help you put this plan together — so if you haven't downloaded it yet, here's the link: www.lovebasedonlinemaketing.com/workbook

Remember, your Online Marketing Plan consists of three parts:

💜 Strategies to find and attract your ideal prospects online.

💜 Strategies (mostly virtual) to begin and nurture a relationship with your ideal prospects.

💜 Strategies (mostly virtual) to inspire and invite your ideal prospects to become ideal clients.

Now, your Marketing Love Factor is at the heart of finding and attracting clients online along with the nurturing strategies.

That's why I'm providing details about each Marketing Love Factor, and how it fits into either client attraction and/or client nurturing, below. (The strategies to inspire and invite them to become clients are the selling campaigns, which I cover in Chapter 7. Those should ideally be combined with a variety of supporting long- and short-term strategies, covered in Chapter 8.)

Marketing Love Factor — Live Q&A, Coaching Calls, or a "Makeover" Radio Show

💜 The live Q&A/Coaching Calls: I have known entrepreneurs who have regularly hosted live Q&A/Coaching calls to their community, which is a great way to nurture your community. The added "bonus" to this strategy is that you can also advertise it outside of your community, as a list-building technique. (You put up an opt-in page so folks have to reserve their spot if they want to join the call, and boom — you're collecting contact information from new leads.)

💙 Hosting a "makeover" radio show (which you can then convert into a podcast for later episodes) is a great vehicle for attracting ideal prospects. Don't forget to always end with a CTA to get your freebie, so you also continuously build your list/community.

Now, you may also want to augment these strategies with written communication to nurture your community even more — offer simple tips, or articles with valuable content that you send to your list regularly (especially if you are hosting live Q&A calls as you won't want to host a call a week, but you really should send out some sort of content each week). And don't worry — it should be fairly easy for you to do so, as all you need to do is transcribe your calls or shows, and find a content writer to craft the copy for you.

Marketing Love Factor — Speaking on Big Stages

This is a fabulous way to not only get yourself and your message in front of new people, but also to make immediate sales. When you speak on stage, your ideal prospects move through the know, like and trust factors much more quickly than when they go through a virtual campaign.

The downside, of course, is lining up those speaking gigs (that takes a certain amount of marketing in and of itself) and you'll need to have a nurture campaign in place for the folks who join your community through the speaking gig. Bonus tip: If you love speaking, you may want to also consider doing a podcast and sending your community links to listen to your latest release as it becomes available.

Marketing Love Factor — Speaking in Front of Small, Intimate Groups

Everything above related to speaking on big stages applies here, except clearly, you're going to need to book more of these talks in order to get in front of the same number of people. On the flip side, however, there are a lot more of these gigs available out there, so it will likely be easier than you think to line them up. Bonus Tip: Reach out to your affiliates and/or Joint Venture partners for opportunities to get in front of their communities, if you offer a similar service/product.

Marketing Love Factor — Being Interviewed

This is a great way to get in front of new audiences and attract new people into your community. And the best part? There certainly seems like a never-ending slew of opportunities to be interviewed, with all the different podcasts and radio shows popping up out there.

Now, it can feel a little daunting to line up gigs when you're first starting out, but many times once you start being interviewed, the invitations start to flow. (Note: This only works if you're a good interviewee.) Networking is also always a good place to start. I also recommend that you look for podcasts that seem like a good fit for you, and then contact the host to be considered as an interviewee. (Note: It's also important to follow directions when you're applying to be interviewed, so fill out the form and do exactly as they ask. When you skip steps in the process, you risk being disqualified.)

Wondering what the difference is between this strategy, and speaking on teleclasses? Well, I separated them because being interviewed is very different than giving a talk. And while yes, there are teleclasses that feel more like interviews, you can also line up teleclasses where you basically give your Signature Talk, and the host either just lets you talk freely, or occasionally pipes in with some canned questions.

So, if answering questions on the fly and having an informal conversation with someone is something you enjoy, definitely looking for these type of interview opportunities — versus those where you're giving more of a one-sided virtual talk.

Now, you'll probably need to come up with something else for additional nurturing, that covers different content to increase the know, like, trust factor. You may want to try hosting your own podcast or radio show, and provide links to your show episodes to your community.

Bonus Tip: Be careful about how often you send your community to opt in for other people's content, as it is counterproductive as your main nurturing strategy.

Marketing Love Factor — Speaking on Teleclasses

See above. In addition, look for opportunities where you can simply share your Signature Talk, versus being interviewed.

Marketing Love Factor— Hosting Your Own Radio Show or Podcast

This can be a fabulous way to find new prospects, and to nurture your existing community.

If you want to use your podcast or radio show to find new prospects, you'll of course need to market your show. If it's on iTunes, launching it correctly is important, and I recommend getting some expert help to do so.

Once it's launched, it's important to consistently promote it (keep in mind, it's pretty easy to promote for free on the various social networking sites).

For your Online Marketing Plan, you'll definitely want to include some marketing tasks related to show promoting.

Marketing Love Factor — Writing Books

Writing books is technically NOT a strategy around which to build your Online Marketing Plan, because you need to market your books in order to get anywhere with them.

However, if you really want to write books, there ARE ways you can set yourself up so that Amazon does the marketing for you (i.e., writing a series, and using Amazon's tools for promoting one in the series each month).

That said, people who buy and read books tend to be buyers of information, so they'll typically invest in higher-end products and programs. So be sure to offer a gift within the book that requires folks to opt in to receive it, so you continue to build your list/community. (Alternatively, you can offer the book for free as an opt in, and build your list/community that way.)

You'll also definitely need to have a nurturing campaign in place, so writing articles/blog posts/a monthly newsletter or hosting a podcast (if you can't write any more than you already are every day) may be strategies to look into for content for your nurturing campaign.

Marketing Love Factor — Writing Articles, Blog Posts, Newsletters

If this is your Marketing Love Factor, congratulations! You can definitely use this particular strategy to attract AND nurture your ideal prospects.

For attraction, you probably want to set up a blog — however, it's not as easy as the "build it and they will come" concept. You need to set up your blog so it actually attracts prospects, typically through SEO and promoting your content via social media. (Some of this can be done automatically every time you post.)

But your own blog isn't the only way you can market yourself. You can also submit articles to digital magazines, ezines, as guest blog posts and more.

For nurturing, you can start your own ezine that goes out at least once a month to your community, or you can send out simple correspondence with tips, or a link to a specific post on your blog.

Marketing Love Factor — Hosting a Television Show

As you can imagine, hosting a television show is a great way to attract new prospects and build a community. However, unless you host it on your YouTube channel (or Google Hangouts or Blab or Periscope or any of the other video streaming services out there), it's going to take a certain amount of work to actually get your show aired on someone else's channel (either a network, or somewhere like Hulu or Netflix).

Now, if you *are* using YouTube or one of those other services to host your show, you'll need to work in promoting (just like your own blog or podcast or book) if you want your show to attract new prospects.

If you want to use the show to nurture your existing community, you can do that too, by sending a link in an email so they can check it out.

Marketing Love Factor — Video

Similar to writing articles, you can use videos in a variety of ways to attract new prospects and nurture your existing community. You can host videos on your own YouTube channel, you can post them on Facebook, Instagram, and on your own blog ... you can even start a video podcast.

If you want to use videos to attract new prospects, keep in mind you'll need to do additional promoting of the actual videos (like posting on social media sites).

Marketing Love Factor — Social Networking

Social networking is definitely more about client attracting than nurturing. While it's true that you can certainly build relationships on social networking sites by connecting with folks and sharing your expertise, you're also "playing in other people's sandboxes," so to speak. Plus, it's a bit risky; if something were to happen with, say, Facebook (or maybe something happens to your account on Facebook), you could lose all your connections.

This is why I personally like to attract new leads from Facebook and other social networking platforms, and then ask them to actually give me their contact information and permission to email them through an opt in. (At that point, you'd need some other ways to nurture your community. You may find that simply sharing what's going on in your life and connecting that way works for you instead of always needing to share content.)

A couple other things to keep in mind about social networking platforms: A) There's an awful lot of them out there and B) It's impossible to be fully engaged on all of them. (Especially if you have other demands on your time, such as say running a business or even something really crazy … like sleeping.)

I like to encourage people to pick a favorite or two, and focus most of their energy on those. Ideally, the platform you choose will not only be enjoyable for YOU, but it will also be the one your ideal prospects are active on, as well.

Marketing Love Factor — Social Networking with an Emphasis on Commenting on Blogs and in Online Groups

A lot of what I said in the "Social Networking" section above applies here as well, but in addition, you may also want to look at platforms such as Tumblr, where you can share and engage in commentary around other people's content. Facebook, LinkedIn and Google+ have quite a bit of content sharing, as well.

Marketing Love Factor — Twitter

I know quite a number of folks who adore the quick conversations that occur on Twitter, and who have found clients just by reaching out to folks and chatting on this platform. If you're someone who enjoys starting conversations and chatting with people online, Twitter may be a perfect focus for you.

(Again, the idea is to start the conversation on Twitter, and then get them to join your community via opting in for a free gift of yours. Then, make sure they receive a nurture campaign of some sort.)

Marketing Love Factor — Publicity or Public relations

This most definitely is all about attracting clients, with the added benefit of boosting your credibility when you're able to add news logos to your site. However, there's really nothing here for client nurturing, so if you choose to add client nurturing to this strategy, you'll need to look into one of the other Factors, as well.

Marketing Love Factor — Networking Groups

Just like publicity/public relations, this one is all about client attracting and nothing to do with client nurturing. However, the other benefit of meeting people face-to- face in a networking group is that it's going to be MUCH easier for you to invite them to become clients. (People want to do business with people they know, like and trust — and by meeting you face-to-face and knee-to-knee, they'll feel like they really know you much more quickly.)

Marketing Love Factor — Internet Marketing

If this one is you, you probably really love "geeking out" about conversion strategies and tips — and you may find yourself saying things like "Oh, this color of red for a headline gets more clicks then this color; isn't that cool?"

The benefit of this strategy is that you'll likely have a built-in advantage to growing your list using SEO strategies and paid online advertising, because along with "geeking out" about conversion strategies, you probably also love learning the latest technical strategy. You'll have an advantage when it comes to actually selling your products and services to your community/list.

However, you probably also aren't terribly into nurturing your community/list, so you may find yourself burning through emails more than one of the other Factors. If you can also bring yourself to provide content for your community/list on a regular basis (through something like a newsletter) or hire a team to do it for you, you'll probably really rock it.

* * *

Okay, so now you may be wondering how all of this comes together to create a consistent Online Marketing Plan that you can follow straight to results.

Before we move to creating the plan itself, let's wrap this up with just a few more tips.

ADDITIONAL TIPS AND EXTRAS:

- Ideally, you "should" be doing SOME sort of promotion once a week, MINIMALLY (if not every day). BUT, when I say promotion, I'm not talking about anything big and complicated, like shooting a 30-minute video, posting it and then sending traffic to it via a whole slew of tweets and posts.

I'm talking about maybe spending 10 minutes on Facebook writing a few content and/or personality-driven posts, with *one* promotional post somewhere in the mix. (See examples of what this could look like later in this chapter.)

❤ I encourage you to take a few minutes *before you start your marketing activities for the day, every day*, to make sure your mindset is in love and abundance. (Check out the Appendix for specific ideas for how to do that, and if you want to take what you see there even deeper, my up-and-coming Love-Based Money and Mindset book may be exactly what you were looking for, so watch for that in August 2016.)

Remember — this is SO important — if your mindset is based in fear and scarcity, and you're worried about money, it will be difficult (if not impossible) to market yourself in a love-based way, so the more you can shift your mindset before you start your marketing activities, the better.

❤ I'd also like to invite you to check in with what Jeanna Gabellini calls your Inner Business Advisor. (More from Jeanna in the Resources section at the end of the book.)

In a nutshell, after you've taken a few moments to ground yourself in a mindset focused on love and abundance, check in with your Inner Business Advisor (IBA) and ask your IBA what you should be focusing on that day for your business and your marketing. (Warning — you may not always get a message about working on your business. Sometimes, the best thing you can do for yourself is to receive whatever comes, which sometimes can be things like taking a walk or reading a book. Really!)

* * *

Before you begin filling in your Online Marketing Plan, let's do a quick recap: the strategies you use to begin and nurture a relationship with a new ideal prospect are considered your online marketing foundation. Then, you create a website and free gift, and a method for nurturing your list — regularly — with content. Finally, your marketing plan typically includes launches of some type (selling products or services or both) combined with various long- and short-term marketing strategies to invite your ideal prospects to become ideal clients.

An important note: You'll notice the plan includes a "Monthly Cash Infusion" strategy. That's because, when you work out your monthly plan, I also want you to think through how you're planning on making money that month. Are you doing a launch? Having a sale? Speaking at an event where you're able to make an offer? Or did you need X number of strategy sessions to land X number of new clients? (And even if you feel like you're at capacity with clients, attracting a few strategy sessions each month will give you a buffer if you do lose a client or two and want to keep the money flowing.)

Part of your monthly marketing activities should go to supporting your Monthly Cash Infusion strategy.

Okay, now it's time to create your plan!

CREATE YOUR ONLINE MARKETING PLAN

(Remember, you can print out the Workbook here, which has plenty of room to fill in your plan: www.lovebasedonlinemaketing.com/workbook)

Fill in the following to the best of your ability, based on the work you've done so far. I've also included examples to help you plan out your own marketing activities.

Your Marketing Love Factor (see Chapter 5):

Your Freebie/CTA (i.e. including all the different urls that have opt-in pages for your gift). Use this space to actually write your freebie, as well as the links that you'll use to direct people to the freebie, so it's all in one place. See Chapter 6):

Secondary Strategies to Attract Your Ideal Prospects to Your Business (these are strategies you're using in addition to your Marketing Love Factor — so for instance, let's say your MLF is blogging. You can easily add a secondary strategy such as promoting those blog posts on social networking platforms. Think of these strategies and tactics as support for your overall MLF — ensuring it's as successful as it can be. See Chapter 8.):

Monthly Cash Infusion Strategy (your cash flow strategy for each month. Examples include launches, sales, strategy sessions, sales calls. See Chapter 7.):

Daily Online Marketing Strategies (Primarily Attraction. Example — your MLF is blogging and your goal is to post 2-3 articles a week. So, perhaps each day you spend time writing plus you spend 10-15 minutes posting your blog posts on social networking sites in addition to writing some nurturing social networking posts. This way, you're not just posting your blog and nothing else. See Chapter 5.):

Weekly Nurturing Marketing Strategies (Primarily Nurturing. Example — you put together your content email around one of your blog posts to send to your list/community or you prep an ezine to send to your community. See Chapter 6.)

Monthly Marketing Strategies (Primarily Inviting. Example — your goal is 10 strategy sessions a month so you get 2 new clients. Keep an eye on how many strategy sessions are coming in, and if it's on the low side, you may want to send out an email or do some additional social networking posts or maybe even some advertising to book those sessions. See Chapters 7-8.)

Special Events: (This category is for anything out of the ordinary marketing-wise. For instance, maybe you're attending an event, or you're speaking at an event one time. You want to make a note of this so you can track what happens along with making sure your other marketing activities support it.)

Woohoo!

If you've filled out each section as best you can, you now have a working Online Marketing Plan.

Congratulations!

Chapter 10
YOUR NEXT STEPS

If there's one final bit of advice I can leave you with, it's this:

Your Online Marketing Plan WILL change.

The important thing is to get something down on paper that will act as a guide for your marketing.

My suggestion is to put a plan together, test it out and see how it goes; then, adjust it accordingly. You don't have to spend a lot of time adjusting it, either — maybe just a few minutes at the start of each month ... but the better prepared you are when you start the month off, the more likely you'll start growing your business.

As your business evolves, your Online Marketing Plan needs to evolve with it. That may mean scaling up, so you can keep up with the growth ... or it may mean doing something completely different if you find the focus of your business changing. (And there's nothing wrong with that — sometimes things happen in our lives that cause us to make a massive shift in our businesses, and that's okay. It's all part of the process.)

So, I really don't want you to agonize about your Online Marketing Plan. I want you to do your best to put something together that fits you right now — your current business level, your goals, your lifestyle and most of all, what you enjoy doing.

You can always tweak it later as you get clearer on what you want to build, and the direction you want to go.

Lastly, if you ever find yourself procrastinating around your marketing, or getting sick a lot, or there's something else going on that's keeping you from reaching your goals, realize you may have uncovered another mindset block. Just like your Online Marketing Plan will change and evolve over time, mindset blocks will also rise to the surface as you continue to work through your challenges. So be patient with yourself, and know if something is showing up, it's likely a sign you've transformed yourself to a point where you can now work through it.

You've got this.

***

If the concept of love-based online marketing resonates with you, I would love to see you put it into practice in your business.

This includes:

- 💜 Loving your marketing.

- 💜 Creating marketing practices that bring your clients in with love.

- 💜 Attracting clients who love you — and who love how you've brought them into your business — with love.

The more business owners who choose to follow this philosophy, the more we can shift the current negative view of online marketing.

It's not going to happen overnight (remember traditional direct response marketing and copy didn't happen overnight either), but if we keep breathing and keep moving forward, it WILL start to shift.

By working together, we truly can make a difference.

XXXOO

Appendix
GLOSSARY

Branding/Taglines/Logos — I define branding as the overall feeling people have around your business, which is usually based on their experience with it. It includes things like (but is not limited to) logos and taglines. Logos are graphical representations of your business while taglines are brief word descriptions.

Calls to Action (CTA) — A call to action is exactly that — you're making a call for people to take action. It could be to buy something, it could be to send an email, it could be to fill out a form, it could be to click on a link or give you an email address, etc. There are lots and lots of different types of CTAs, but the most important thing to remember is you MUST include one if you're writing direct response copy and using direct response marketing.

Community/List — "List" basically refers to a list of folks who you can contact — in many cases it's a list of email addresses. But as the word "list" is dehumanizing, as much as possible, I try to bring the word "community" in — community/list — as a constant reminder that there are humans on the other end of those email addresses. As much as possible, I try to bring the word community in — community/list — as a constant reminder that there are humans on the other end of those email addresses.

In addition, "community" is all-encompassing. Your promotional efforts can be much bigger than simply a list of emails you have permission to mail to. Your community includes your Twitter and

Facebook friends, blog readers, podcast listeners, video watchers, etc. Really, anyone who is following you (no matter what medium they choose) is part of your community.

Conversions — The holy grail of direct response — direct response copy lives and dies by conversion rate. Conversion rate refers to the percentage of folks who read your copy and take the desired action (i.e. how many visitors to your website give you their email address, how many people who read your sales letter buy your product, etc.) Conversion rates vary depending upon what you're asking people to do (i.e. click on a link in an email, give you their email address or get out their credit card to buy something). For instance, a good conversion rate for a sales letter is 1% — that means 1 out of every 100 people who visit your sales letter buy.

If you're asking folks to do something that's free (i.e. give you their email address in exchange for something like a special report or webinar) you should have a higher conversion rate than 1%, but there's a huge variation because there are so many other factors. In some cases, you might see 20%-30% conversions on opt ins (i.e. using a paid Facebook ad campaign that sends new "colder" visitors to your website, who may never have heard of you before so they may be less likely to opt-in for your freebie) to 60% or higher (i.e. having an affiliate/JV partner send an email to their list or you send an email to your list to an opt-in page, because the people who click on those links are much warmer as they would have some sort of relationship with you or your affiliate/JV partner, so they are more likely to opt in).

Emails — Emails (or electronic mail) can be used for all sorts of things — staying in touch with old friends, communicating with clients, or marketing to your ideal prospects. In love-based copywriting, I like to think of emails as sales representatives who direct your ideal prospects to the perfect department (i.e. sales letter) for them.

Ideal Clients/Ideal Prospects — Here in the land of love-based copywriting, we prefer the terms "Ideal Clients" for customers and "Ideal Prospects" for leads. As much as possible, try not to use terms that depersonalize your prospect (like "list").

Joint Venture (aka JVs) and Affiliates — These are folks who promote your products and services and you pay them a commission for every sale. The difference between Joint Venture and affiliates typically is the level of promotion and commitment — Joint Venture partners typically act more like partners and the two of you will work harder to promote each other to your respective communities, whereas affiliates are typically less committed to you and the promotion.

Love-Based Business — A business built on the foundation of love and love-based emotions, which includes marketing, selling, and delivering products and services via love-based emotions (versus triggering fear-based emotions). In addition, a love-based business also means YOU love your business as much as your business loves YOU — so a love-based business also needs to built around exactly what YOU want for your biz and life (i.e. your goals, preferences and life).

Marketing — A "blanket" term encompassing everything involved in the experience your ideal client/prospect has when it comes to your business. This includes everything from a broad range overview of how you're going to get new clients into your business, to the tiniest of details, like how you invoice, or your customer service team follow-up. However, when most people talk about marketing, what they're really talking about is some form of marketing communications. For the purposes of this book, I define marketing as the strategies you use to attract your ideal prospects, nurture the relationship, and then invite them to become clients.

Marketing Plan — A way to organize and schedule your marketing activities (ideally, it's laid out in such a way that if you follow your plan, you'll reach your goals).

Marketing Resistance — Unconscious or subconscious blocks that stop you from marketing yourself and your business successfully.

Online Marketing — Marketing strategies that predominantly take place via the Internet.

Opt-in Page/Landing Page/Squeeze Page — All of these titles refer to the exact same thing: a page that asks for a name and email in exchange for something free. If you're offering a free call or webinar, or a special report pdf, or a recording of a training (or any other type of free offer), you would likely use an opt-in page to collect information.

Here in love-based copywriting land, I prefer the term "opt-in page" (which is the term we'll use throughout this book) because it best reflects the actual process: your ideal prospects choose to give you their contact info and start a relationship with you. (Squeeze page in particular is a very manipulative term, as it refers to the page "squeezing" the contact information out of people.) I also like to think of opt-in pages as the "line outside your online showroom."

PLC — Product Launch Content. This is part of the Product Launch Formula. Basically, the Product Launch Formula begins by giving away 3 pieces of content (PLCs) which is how buzz and excitement are built around launching a product.

PLF — Product Launch Formula. Jeff Walker created the Product Launch Formula, which is a specific formula best suited for selling an information product or program.

Product Launch — An event created to sell a product or program. In many cases, the launch is carefully constructed to create a significant amount of buzz around the product, so customers are excited to buy.

Sales Letters (also knows as long-copy sales letters or long-form sales letters) — These are those super-long pages on the Internet where you scroll down for what seems like forever looking for the price.

Now, in the land of love-based copywriting, I want you to think about these online sales letters as "departments" in your online showroom, because these pages are how you sell specific products, programs, events, etc.

Website — The "official" definition is a collection of web pages that lives on the Internet and provides a broad overview of your business.

However, here in love-based copywriting land, we shift that definition a bit. Here, a website is an "online showroom" so you have an online place to attract, inspire and invite your ideal prospects to visit and see if they want to become your ideal clients.

APPENDIX — EXERCISES TO HELP YOU SHIFT YOUR MINDSET FROM FEAR TO LOVE

Any exercise that can help you expand, open up and feel abundant will work to help you shift your mindset. So, for instance, exercises that tap into the Law of Attraction can work really well here.

Following are a few areas you can focus on, to get started:

- Gratitude (make lists of what you feel grateful for and really feel into being grateful) — Gratitude is one of the most powerful ways to move into an abundant mindset, because if you're feeling grateful, it's pretty much impossible to feel scarcity or lack at the same time. And, if you can even feel grateful for a few minutes, it's possible to completely shift your mindset to abundance. (And if you're reading this book, I can almost guarantee you have something to be grateful for — even if your business is looking a bit grim, if you have a place to stay and food in your fridge and clothes to wear, you can just start there.)

- Meditation — Meditation has the ability to shift your brain chemistry, which can help you with all sorts of things, from making it easier to work through your mindset blocks, to actually moving into an abundant mindset.

- ♥ Journaling — Journaling is great for working through issues and blocks, so if you're feeling stuck in lack or scarcity, journaling may help you work through your feelings so you can finally release them.

- ♥ Affirmations — Affirmations can help you focus on abundance and love. They should always be written in the present and be positive — i.e. "I effortlessly attract abundance into my life."

- ♥ Rituals to cleanse old energy that is no longer serving you and welcome in new energy — This is particularly good to do if you've experienced a big shift or breakthrough. You'll want to clear out that old energy that lingers from before your breakthrough.

- ♥ Grounding — stand outside in your bare feet touching earth and relax. (Stand on the ground for at least 10 minutes — skin needs to be touching the earth. You may want to listen to some music you enjoy as you do this.) This is a great way to safely release any energy that isn't serving you. So, for example, if you're feeling a lot of anxiety, and you do this, you may discover you start to feel calmer and more balanced.

If you want to learn more about shifting your mindset, you may want to check out my "Love-Based Money and Mindset" book coming soon (www.Lovebasedcopybooks.com).

About the Author
MICHELE PW

Considered one of the hottest direct response copywriters and marketing consultants in the industry today, Michele PW (Michele Pariza Wacek) has a reputation for crafting copy and creating online and offline marketing campaigns that get results.

Michele started writing professionally in 1992, working at agencies and on staff as a marketing/communication/

writing specialist. In 1998, she started her business as a freelance copywriter.

But she quickly realized her vision was bigger than serving her clients as a one-woman-shop. In 2004, she began the transformation to building a copywriting company.

Two years later, her vision turned into reality. The Love-Based Copywriting and Marketing Company is the premiere direct response copywriting and marketing company today, catering to entrepreneurs and small business owners internationally, including the "Who's Who" of Internet Marketing.

In addition, Michele is also a national speaker and author and has completed two novels. She holds a double major in English and Communications from the University of Wisconsin-Madison. Currently she lives in the mountains of Prescott, Arizona with her husband Paul and her 2 dogs — border collie Nick and southern squirrel hunter Cassie.

Resources

"Love-Based Online Marketing" (Volume 3 in the Love-Based Business Series) **Companion Workbook** — Get it here: www.lovebasedonlinemaketing.com/workbook

"Map to Profits" — Jeanna Gabellini's gift to you. If you want to design a business that makes you say, "HELL YES! I love what I'm doing, the way I'm doing it and my profits have increased substantially," download this visual map of how Jeanna tripled her income in less than a year — with ease and FUN! You're also going to get your own visual map to fill in with your most important "HELL YES'" for this year. (**If it's not a HELL YES, it doesn't go on your map!**) Jeanna designed this map to make your next profitable steps very clear. Download it here: http://lovebasedonlinemarketing.com/jeanna

"Blind Spot to Brilliance: Marketing from the Inside Out" eBook — Therese Skelly's gift to you. If you long to find your message, and get it out into the world, this workbook-style eBook **will show you all the elements of what Therese calls "Inner Marketing" — the work you need to do BEFORE you start the tactical marketing. If you can't articulate what's unique about you, or you sound a bit like everyone else....you will lose money!** But more importantly, you will not get to do the great work you are "supposed" to, in the world. Therese designed this eBook to ask you lots of questions, to get you thinking and going deeper than you have before with your branding and messaging. Download it here: http://lovebasedonlinemarketing.com/therese

Need tech help? Email info@michelepw.com, let us know what you're looking for, and we'll be in touch to discuss how we can best assist you.

OTHER BOOKS BY MICHELE PW

"Love-Based Copywriting Method: The Philosophy Behind Writing Copy That Attracts, Inspires and Invites" (Volume 1 in the Love-Based Business Series) — Learn more at www.LoveBasedCopyBooks.com

"Love-Based Copywriting System: A Step-by-Step Process to Master Writing Copy that Attracts, Inspires and Invites (Volume 2 in the Love-Based Business Series) — Learn more at www.LoveBasedCopyBooks.com

"The Dirty Little Secret About Direct Response/Internet Marketing: Why What You've Been Taught Isn't Working for You and What You Can Do to Turn it Around" — Learn more at www.LoveBasedCopyBooks.com

"5 Mistakes Entrepreneurs and Small Business Owners Make When They Hire a Copywriter and How to Avoid Them. PLUS 10 Questions You Should Ask/Tasks You Should Do BEFORE You Hire a Copywriter" — Learn more at www.LoveBasedCopyBooks.com

"Holiday Marketing Secrets — How to Grow Your Biz YearRound (And yes, these strategies can help you build a

more successful and profitable biz no matter what time of year it is)" — Learn more at www.LoveBasedCopyBooks.com

"Love-Based Marketing"

Book by Susan Liddy — "Love-Based Marketing: The No Sell-Out, Copy-Out, Burn-Out Method to Attract Your Soul Mate Clients into Your Business" — Learn more at www.SusanLiddy.com

Now that you know all about the Love-Based Marketing and Copywriting philosophy, are you ready to write the copy for your marketing materials in a way that attracts, nurtures and invites your ideal prospects to become ideal clients?

OR WOULD YOU LIKE US TO DO IT FOR YOU?

DONE-FOR-YOU COPYWRITING SERVICES — GET MORE LEADS, CLIENTS AND SALES WITHOUT DOING THE WORK YOURSELF!

As a busy entrepreneur or small business owner, you're probably looking for ways to leverage your time and money. Well, there's no better leverage than direct response copywriting.

Consider this — copywriting leverages your marketing and your selling. You can make money without picking up the phone and selling one-on-one. (Imagine the time saving right there.) You can easily add multiple streams of income to your business. You can turn your website into a lead-generation tool so you have a consistently full pipeline of clients. You can send out an email or a direct mail piece and watch money flow into your business!

That's the beauty of direct response copywriting.

But there's only one small problem — if you want results, you need to be trained. And, as a busy entrepreneur or small business owner, who has time for training?

That's why I'd like to introduce you to the Michele PW Done-For-You Copywriting Services. Whether you're looking for a one-shot copy project (like getting your website written or a few emails or a postcard) or an entire project launch campaign, or a combination of copywriting and marketing strategy, our team of trained copywriters and marketing strategists can take care of your needs and (even more importantly) get you the results you're looking for.

Want to learn more? Just email or call for the details — Info@MichelePW.com or (toll free) 877-754-3384 X2.

(Note — we also write articles, press releases, social networking posts and more. Just ask if you want to learn more.)

TESTIMONIALS

"Working with Michele PW was such a relief because she GETS direct response copywriting. She knew what I was looking for and was able to deliver. With her help, we had record-breaking numbers for one of our campaigns. I highly recommend Michele if you're looking for copywriting that gets you results."

Ali Brown
Founder of Alexandria Brown International
www.AlexandriaBrown.com

"With Michele's copywriting and social networking help, I had my BIGGEST 6-figure launch ever! And I'm no stranger to 6-figure product launches. Before Michele, I had 5 6-figure launches. But this one I did with Michele blew all the other ones away. We more than doubled what I had done before. Plus, even though I knew the launch was on track, there were moments I panicked because I wasn't staying up until 2 a.m. writing copy. I highly recommend Michele, especially if you're getting ready to launch a new product or service."

Lisa Sasevich
The Queen of Sales Conversion
www.LisaSasevich.com

"I've had the pleasure of working with some of the top marketing minds of our time, and as far as results are concerned, Michele is right there with them. One idea she gave me for one of my recent launches, directly resulted in a 30% increase of sales. I'm planning on implementing that idea on a regular basis the results were so powerful. Thanks Michele!"

Mark Harris
Co-Founder www.ThoughtLeaderSecrets.com

"With Michele's expert copywriting and marketing help, we're averaging an 8% conversion rate! Considering that 1% is typically considered really good by industry standards, we were blown away by the results."

Linda H. Hunt
Owner
www.sumsolutions.com

"Thanks to your eagle eye and copywriting changes to ONE simple email I increased registrations for my "Give Your Pricing a Kick-in-the-Pants" Virtual Workshop Intensive by 20%! That's money that went straight into my bank account!"

Kendall SummerHawk
The "Horse Whisperer for Business"
Author, "How to Charge What You're Worth and Get It!"
www.KendallSummerHawk.com

Made in the USA
San Bernardino, CA
24 April 2016